THE SOUL OF LEARNING

The Soul of Learning is a groundbreaking book that bridges together cultural work, contemplative practices, and ancient scriptures. Inside each chapter, readers are challenged and inspired to come face to face with themselves as they encounter teachers in all forms—from spiritual sages to critical theorists, from prophets to poets, from hip-hop rappers to reggae artists. This book is multifaceted and multidisciplinary. It models the essence of education by offering multiple entry points into holistic learning: somatic, aesthetic, emotional, intellectual, ethical, relational, and spiritual.

The Soul of Learning embodies a pedagogical disruption in pursuit of personal sovereignty. What process must we go through to reimagine ourselves in relation to each other and the world around us? This book offers a semblance of an answer. As a way to bring the sacred into schooling, Keator and Watson courageously connect spirituality, activism, and education through curated readings, guided activities, and intentional exercises. It's a ready-to-go syllabus and hands-on workbook all in one! Altogether this book is revelatory and provides innovative ways to teach and learn, lead and live. *The Soul of Learning* documents a transformative journey, through the interiority of our being into a revolutionary call for collective belonging.

Mary Keator, Ph.D., is the founder of Healthy Integrated Living (healthyintegrated living.com), offering a customized wellness plan to bring balance, integration, and well-being into life and work. She is also the author of Lectio Divina as Contemplative Pedagogy a resource for educators interested in learning how to integrate contemplative practices into their teaching methodology.

Vajra M. Watson is a scholar activist, faculty director, and professor of educational leadership and racial justice in the College of Education at Sacramento State University. She has over twenty years of experience as a teacher, community organizer, and researcher. She received her doctorate from the Graduate School of Education at Harvard University.

THE SOUL OF LEARNING

rituals of awakening, magnetic pedagogy, and living justice

Mary Keator and Vajra M. Watson

NEW YORK AND LONDON

First published 2022
by Routledge
605 Third Avenue, New York, NY 10158

and by Routledge
2 Park Square, Milton Park, Abingdon, Oxon, OX14 4RN

Routledge is an imprint of the Taylor & Francis Group, an informa business

© 2022 Mary Keator and Vajra M. Watson

The right of Mary Keator and Vajra M. Watson to be identified as authors of this work has been asserted by them in accordance with sections 77 and 78 of the Copyright, Designs and Patents Act 1988.

All rights reserved. No part of this book may be reprinted or reproduced or utilised in any form or by any electronic, mechanical, or other means, now known or hereafter invented, including photocopying and recording, or in any information storage or retrieval system, without permission in writing from the publishers.

Trademark notice: Product or corporate names may be trademarks or registered trademarks, and are used only for identification and explanation without intent to infringe.

Library of Congress Cataloging-in-Publication Data
A catalog record for this book has been requested

ISBN: 978-1-032-05346-2 (hbk)
ISBN: 978-1-032-05345-5 (pbk)
ISBN: 978-1-003-19716-4 (ebk)

DOI: 10.4324/9781003197164

Typeset in Bembo
by Apex CoVantage, LLC

~♡~

To YOU, the Reader,

May you experience the generative power of silence and the magnetic power of love in your learning, teaching and living.

Namasté
Mary

~♡~

i dedicate this book to your inner light. all that we do and who we are is connected; i pray this offering is useful.
~vajra mujiba watson

CONTENTS

Foreword   ix
    Charles Scott
Preface   xii

1   Meditation on Education   1

2   Silence   11

3   Just Breathe   20

4   Mental Emancipation   30

5   Expanding Perspectives   48

6   The Journey Into Truth   60

7   Into the Heart of Healing   73

8   Teaching Toward Sovereignty   91

9   Beloved Community   106

10 Ancient Futures	118
Afterword	*128*
Hodari Bayano Davis	
References	*131*
Index	*136*

FOREWORD

This book is a radical text. A radical text for students, which all of us are.

In my 15 years at Simon Fraser University, I continue to see a pattern. Many students are consumed by grades and securing high-paying jobs.

Honestly, I find this sad. Truly sad. But the good news is that such a conversation provides a perfect opportunity about "What really counts in life" or "What do you want to do with your (one wild and precious) life, and why?" It almost always happens that we have some great conversations, electric with excitement. I find the students are silently hungering for them. Over the years several students have told me, "You're the first person in my entire life who has ever asked me these questions and allowed these explorations! Thank you!"

Again, this is sad. I am the first to ask these questions? That is the result of an education system, in the context of secular and neo-liberalized society, that thinks our inner lives—purpose, meaning, inner peace, an inner sense of connection—do not have a place in learning. This radical book, on the other hand, with a title that includes the phrase "the soul of learning," allows these kinds of explorations; indeed, this book is made to create them.

Mary Keator and Vajra M. Watson are taking you on a journey—one might call it *the* journey—and each station along the way is carefully considered. This book is radical because, as the word implies, it returns to the root of education: these spiritual essentials of life. Just as all of us have bodies, minds, and emotions, we also all have a spiritual dimension to our beings.

See if you can relate to any of these dimensions of spirituality:

- finding meaning, purpose, and joy in life;
- motivating ideals which give rise to hope;
- appreciating the beauty, aesthetics, and sense of awe and wonder;

- connecting to something larger than oneself, whether it is a human collective or to the more-than-human world, even reaching out to the entire cosmos?

These are all dimensions of spirituality, and we can—and should—develop spiritually.

This is a book about what educators and philosophers refer to as *praxis*, the integration of theory and practice. The soul of learning can be articulated in theory but can only be *realized* through experience. This book offers the perfect balance.

Mary and Vajra begin their preface with a profound truth from the *Isha Upanishad*, but common to all the contemplative traditions, that at once encompasses personal identity and social justice. You are engaging with a book that gives you the tools and the rituals to answer *the* great educational question "Who will you become?" with passion and authority.

This book will offer you a natural progression through the many facets of an educational "experience of the interior and infinite," as the authors phrase it in the first chapter. Contemporary Western, white culture and educational systems have focused on doing and having, but in the various contemplative traditions of East and West, education focused much more on developing the mind and virtue.

The key is how to turn within to connect with the heart. How to dwell in the silence and fullness of the heart. How to let its beat propel us out toward others. This is what Paulo Freire wrote so much about. This heart space is where, as he put it so profoundly in *Pedagogy of the Oppressed*, dialogue becomes an encounter between people, mediated by their experiences in the world, in order for them to name and to claim their worlds.

In this book, Mary and Vajra show us that education is a project of both being and interbeing, these become its beginning, middle, and end. Learning is offered here, as the authors put it, "As a sacred text in direct relationship with the divine text of your life." These curricula can and should appear in every subject area, weaving threads that connect and enlighten.

Education is largely a process of divine remembering. The authors begin with an entire chapter devoted to silence, offering a syllabus of stillness that honors the intimate depths of solitary silence and that inward turn. Those who have experienced these depths of silence know their inward pull, their deepening calm, their expansive, connective power. Yogananda wrote, in his *Metaphysical Meditations*: "My silence, like the ether, passes through everything, carrying the songs of earth, atoms, and stars into the halls of His infinite mansion."[1]

The authors ask: Where is your silence? The contemplative journey begins and has its life in silence. "You lean into silence," as they write, and it slowly comes to embrace you; you sink into its revealing vastness. The Nobel laureate Toni Morrison would tell graduate students that if they wanted to work with her, they were required to find time—minutes, hours, days—to be alone, to have solitude and silence.

Mary and Vajra then invite us to experience mental emancipation: "Teaching towards transformation is circular and prioritizes self-discovery." This is a profound pedagogical point. You cannot fake it here. The understandings developed in these iterative intersubjective contemplative approaches are not only intellectual but also intuitive.

In his essay "What is Education For?" David Orr so wisely wrote, "The plain fact is that the planet does not need more successful people. But it does desperately need more peacemakers, healers, restorers, storytellers, and lovers of every kind. It needs people who live well in their places."[2] We need to find our sources for collective healing. Consider "Pretty Hurts" by Beyoncé and "Where is the Love?" by the Black Eyed Peas.

Vajra and Mary have now established a home for beloved community. From "I" we have moved to "I-and-I," to interdependence, to interbeing, to Indra's Net. There is a profound connection between the unfolding of self to Self through contemplative practices and inclusion, to the recognition and validation of diversity, to the establishment of equity, and to the development of well-being throughout the biosphere.

Nothing is left out of *The Soul of Learning*. We have an integral vision of education that not only includes inner and outer, individual and collective, but also, most important, allows the student to realize, satori-like, the connections between them—the full integral vision. We have, then, not just a theory but a *praxis* of everything.

A final point about what makes this book both so engaging and powerful: its teachings are transmitted largely from the parables and poems—the literature—of the wisdom and contemplative traditions. Many of these stories have been passed down through hundreds of generations. Besides: *who doesn't love a good story?* The wise sages, writers, and artists have known for millennia that stories most effectively transmit the power of sacred teachings. These are now yours to enjoy.

Charles Scott, Ph.D.
Adjunct Professor
Faculty of Education
Simon Fraser University

PREFACE

A Collective Belonging

The inspiration for *The Soul of Learning* came when we were at the base of the Himalayas. During the winter recess of 2019–2020, we were invited by our colleague Dr. Maureen Hall to teach at Dev Sanskriti University in Haridwar, India.[3] One day while walking to the Ganges, we began exploring the beginning lines to *The Isha Upanishad*, "The Lord is enshrined in the hearts of all," and started contemplating the connection between authenticity, educational equity, and spiritual practices.

When we returned from India, we felt a sense of urgency to write this book.

Each of these pages has been written collaboratively in the fullest sense. Even the order of authorship was solely for alphabetical purposes. To accomplish this kind of communal act, we met over Zoom multiple days a week for over a year. During this time, we shared resources over text and email and even snail mailed each other books. We read pieces out loud and waded through the waters of each and every word. Whatever mistakes or mishaps we may have made, we hope it does not diminish from the greater task at hand. *The Soul of Learning: rituals of awakening, magnetic pedagogy and living justice* is our call to arms. Arms that extend from the heart and reach out, grab hold, and do not let go.

We are both professors in the academy with vast K-12 and higher education teaching experience. We have sought ways to manifest learning experiences for ourselves and our students in ways that are authentic and alive. The road has not been easy. The struggle over how to do school is real. Yet each of us got to a point where we stopped asking *What are we fighting against*? and started asking, *Who are we fighting for*? This calling inspires us to work differently in spaces to manifest radical vulnerability and collective accountability.

For us, education is sacred, and every individual is both a student and a teacher. The truth is that each of us is a unique irreplaceable living, breathing being. We are experts of our own lives. The aim of education, in its highest form, is to engage all people to move toward their full potential and actualize their self-worth. From this vantage point, learning is life-giving, experiential in nature, and filled with love. The love we describe does not just flow in one direction but is critical, dynamic, and reciprocal. It is, at its core, relational. This kind of learning and teaching practice requires intention, consistency, joy, and patience. Hard work. Hard heart work. It is multifaceted, exquisitely complex, and glorious all at the same time.

It's hard to imagine that we were strangers less than two years ago. Bringing this book to life forced us to confront ourselves and one another in new ways. It wasn't always pretty, in fact, it was raw, real, and intense. In the spirit of building transparency, we want to pivot deeper inwards. To model this form of opening, we offer insights into ourselves as a way to build trust for this journey toward justice.

This is who we are.

Mary Keator

I am a child of the universe. My ancestral roots extend back to Holland, Ireland, and beyond (dark Irish). The oldest daughter of eight, I grew up in a Christian family in the mountains of western Massachusetts, where I spent hours playing in the woods that surrounded my family home. Life revolved around family needs (10 of us in total), the liturgical calendar, and the teachings of Jesus. Grace before meals. Prayers in the morning and evening. Sunday Mass, Friday fasts. Confession and Communion. Coming of age progressed from Baptism to First Communion to Confirmation. Somewhere along the way, a deep desire to know the other paths to God emerged within me. One day while walking down the street with my father to retrieve the mail, I asked him, "Dad, how can I commit to one religion and be confirmed before I have explored the others? I need to study the different religious traditions first before I can make this important decision."

Although not well received at the time, I quietly continued my own exploration. I began to read sacred texts and world literatures. Moved by these great teachers, I began to explore teaching—I come from a lineage of caring gifted teachers—and received a master's degree in teaching with a concentration in literature. I then began teaching middle school, but I soon left to care for my newborn daughter, Sophia. Just under two years later, my daughter Madeleine arrived. I made a new decision. I chose to stay home to care for them and teach them. Little did I know how much they would teach me. Sophia and Madeleine continue to be two of my greatest teachers.

My life has led me to live in various places in the U.S. and Mexico. While living on the border in El Paso, Texas, I began studying yoga. It was love at first pose. Along my yogic journey, I met Dr. Shyam Singha, my spiritual yoga teacher. Shyam was born in Kashmir, India, in the northern part of the Himalayas. For me, meeting Shyam was like meeting Jesus. He was plugged in and tuned in to a sacred energy that flowed through him in subtle yet extraordinary ways. He not only welcomed everyone to his table; he also fed them food that he himself prepared. "Food is medicine, and medicine is food" was a favorite saying of his. He was an amazing healer, healing all in need. He was also a gifted teacher and left a profound impression on me. He pushed me to continue to question everyone and everything, to live authentically and simply, and not to take life so seriously. I am forever grateful to him.

As I continued to deepen my yogic studies and teaching, I began formally studying religions, gaining a master's degree in theology. During this course of study, I was graced to study under the tutelage of Fr. Warren J. Savage, a compassionate, wise, and soulful being. A man who truly lives, "Love of God and neighbor *as* self." He not only saw gifts within me but also helped me to develop and integrate them into my life. He encouraged me to pursue a Ph.D. and to weave my interests together. I completed a Ph.D. in humanities with a dual concentration in comparative literature and maps to consciousness in the world's religious traditions. My heart continued to expand. Words cannot begin to express my abiding love and gratitude for his steady, loving presence in my life.

While teaching at Dev Sanskriti University, I met two elders in the community, Agamvir and Pushpa Singh. Although I was a stranger to them, they welcomed me into their home as if I was a member of their family. We shared meals, meditated, chanted, and prayed together. Agamvir taught me about the divine magnetism of the gayatri mantra. Their humility, gentleness, and boundless generosity deeply touched my heart. I am forever grateful to them.

I bow in deep reverence to all my teachers, those named and unnamed.

Humility, like humus, is close to the earth.
Sooner or later it becomes a source of fertility and growth.
It allows others to be and accepts its own limits as well as its grandeur.
It is the opening of the Kingdom within oneself.
~ Jean-Yves Le Loup ~

And so, I began manifesting—in communion with others—what had always been hidden within.

I am a contemplative and as such practice rituals to keep me oriented toward the sacred. These rituals (yoga, meditation, chanting, barefoot walking, drumming, and *lectio divina*) help me slow down and experience the fullness of the life-breathing spirit within and around me. Nature. Human beings. Sacred books. Dance. Song. All brimming with the reverence and profundity of life. Alongside my personal practice of *lectio divina*, I have written and presented extensively on *lectio divina* as a form of contemplative pedagogy. It is this contemplative pedagogy and practice, along with my yogic studies and practice, that continues to inform my teaching.

In my courses, I work to create experiential learning opportunities for students to tap into their inner wellspring. For instance, in *Writing about Yoga*, students come to class with their yoga mats in hand, ready to engage in the practice. Peculiar? Maybe. But how are students supposed to write authentically about something they have yet to experience? While reading *The Katha Upanishad* in my world literature course, students stand up and pretend to pull in the reins of their minds and control their sense desires as they steer the chariot of their lives. It is in these embodied learning experiences that the students begin to encounter the wisdom of the authors while sparking their own inner wisdom. I chant and meditate with my students to silence their chattering minds and focus their attention. Together we work to create a more compassionate community. My classroom is filled with life: smiles and laughter, play and purpose, curiosity and queries, and yes, sometimes even tears as students begin to awaken to a deeper truth and surrender their hardened shields.

This book is the fruit of our lives. It came about through hard work; heart work; deep, gritty soul work. During the course of writing it, the world went into shutdown mode. Classrooms closed and moved online. Communities faded behind layers of masks, parks emptied of children playing, and family and friends quarantined behind closed doors. As if this loss was not enough, I too, like many of you reading this book, experienced further loss.

On November 30th, the morning of her seventeenth birthday, our beloved Weimaraner Sunshine passed away. It was Sunshine who taught me the lesson of wild abandon—to embrace life and live it to its fullness. On February 1st, my father, the man who had instilled in me the importance of faith, family, and discipline, breathed his last breath.

Yet in the midst of it all, just as spring has brought forth new buds, new life keeps emerging. I, too, am emerging with a new offering, *The Soul of Learning*, a newly rediscovered soul sister named Vajra Mujiba Watson, who stretched me to think about justice in expanded ways, and a new venture called Healthy Integrated Living (healthyintegratedliving.com). I continue to weave together my passions and purpose to love deeper, inspire others, and live fully awake and alive.

Vajra Mujiba Watson

First and foremost, may I take a moment to formally acknowledge the lineage of teachers who have shaped and informed my work and walk in the world. In the sphere of higher education, I was directly impacted by the lessons shared by Pedro Noguera, Sara Lawrence-Lightfoot, and Mark Warren. As a youth, I was taught (formally and informally) by Hodari B. Davis and Imam Bilal Hyde. For all my days, my greatest teachers have been my parents and my children: Farid and Dara; Tsadiku and Adiyah. I also want to acknowledge my parents' teachers, mainly, Murshid Sam and Hazrat Inayat Khan. I have looked at teaching and learning through the prism of sacred knowledge for as long as I can remember. Even though I learned how to "do school," I also experienced spaces wherein learning was a rupture of growth and an expansion of horizons. There were days I left Mr. Davis' courses in the Black Studies Department at Berkeley High School feeling as if I had just eaten a full meal, like my soul was literally full and beaming from the divine exchange that took place.

As a student and teacher, I have experienced glimpses of what Mary and I are describing in this book. Yet I found it challenging to articulate and piece together. I realized that to understand *The Soul of Learning*, I had to reconnect to my own beginnings. Some of my earliest memories occurred inside The Garden of Bismillah, the name of the communal house in Berkeley where my family and I lived during my first 5 years of my life. I vividly remember the central prayer room, a gathering place for dhikr and meditation.[4] Various religious teachers would pass through The Garden of Bismillah and offer sacred lessons. On Sundays, there was a service called Universal Worship. The first candle lit represents the light of Divine Truth, and from it all the other nine candles are lit to represent major religious traditions such as Buddhism (Divine Compassion), Christianity (Divine Self-Sacrifice), Hinduism (Divine Wisdom), Islam (Divine Unity), Judaism (Divine Law), and Zoroastrianism (Divine Purity). The ninth candle signifies spiritual traditions—known and unknown—that bring us closer to Divine Love.

Although these early experiences shaped my outlook on life, I have not taken much time to revisit them. What I have said over the years is that at an early age, my mom, Dara, would sing angels into the room.

Although we eventually moved out of The Garden of Bismillah, I stayed relatively active in the Sufi community, visiting various temples, mosques, and religious sanctuaries. The absolute beauty of these places, I recall viscerally, is that they all felt familiar and similar. Inside a Buddhist temple, monks were reciting in unison, "Om Mani Padme Hum." As a child listening to this repetitive hymn, the words blended together such that all I heard over and over was "Oh Mommy, Take Me Home." I am grateful to have seen and heard the world through these sacred ceremonies.

But the world is not just sacred; it is also scarred. Filled with scars from the brutalities of injustice. We're sinking inside this mythology of white supremacy. The pain is all too real. I started to get frustrated with some of my Sufi brothers and sisters who live inside the close-knit caverns of community—chanting about harmony—while so many people are starving and the ravages of inequality continue to steal away our humanity.

As much as we need spiritual-based soul surgery, it's also critical to consider who we are in the world. We are the embodiment of our ancestors: good, bad, and otherwise. Our race, class, and gender matter. What does it mean to have a kind of soul surgery with respect to my positionality as a 43-year-old white woman?

Throughout my life, there have been many moments when close friends would tell me, "You're not *really* white" and reference my name, Islamic roots, or multi-cultural upbringing. But I would shake my head and affirm my whiteness. Whether I am covering my hair or have locks, whether my children are Black or not, whether I am given a pass or somehow considered "down," this does not disconnect me—in any way—from all the ways *I am white supremacy*. Every aspect of my life is predicated on a system of oppression that reaffirms my pale skin privileges. It is inescapable, like a fish in water is wet.

Whiteness is the problem. I know this like I know I have bones in my body. It is the architecture of our lives. But let it be known: whiteness is not the solution. And white people—*my people*—we are definitely not the solution. We got race wrong, among other things. We have spent hundreds of years trying to divorce and Other ourselves from *Hue*-manity. It is going to take a lot of intergenerational work to rejoin us with the world. That is if the majority of people on earth, who are overwhelmingly Black, Indigenous, People of Color, will even still accept us.

Toni Morrison was spot on when she told us, "People who practice racism are bereft . . . If you can only be tall because somebody is on their knees, then you have a serious problem. And my feeling is white people have a very, very serious problem, and they should start thinking about what they are going to do about it."[5] Building on Morrison's analysis, most of my scholarship over the past decade has focused on racial justice and transformative schooling. Yet as I come full circle, I see where and how spiritual work can atone in a different way, helping us move from being skin-folk to kin-folk.

I've been thinking a lot about Malcolm X's pilgrimage to Mecca, where he came face to face with pale-skinned people with blue eyes who did not embody racism. This shook him to his core. For these white folks, it seems, submission to GOD brought them peace. And this peace allowed for a soulful recentering to ensue. In other words, the spirit of an individual became stronger than the deleterious race of a people.

Perhaps there is a lesson here about *justice as spiritual practice*.[6]

The world is filled with great, wonderful teachers, and it's such a gift to keep learning. In my last meeting with the vice chancellor of Dev Sanskriti University, Dr. Chinmay Pandya, he said that through meditation, we'd meet with one another again very soon on the astral plane. I have no doubt that his profound energy helped inspire this work. And of course, there's my co-author! Being on this journey with Mary has definitely pushed my understanding and experiences with communion. She helped draw out ideas that were buried deep inside my soul and helped nurture the space for my truth to blossom. Here we are, two white women scholars, reconnecting to a deeper essence of life itself and finding common ground for revolution.

> *There is one question I'd really love to ask.*
> *Is there a place for the hopeless sinner*
> *Who has hurt all man-kind just to save his own?*
> *Believe me. One love, one heart.*
> ~ Bob Marley & The Wailers ~

Our lives connected in Haridwar, India. Haridwar is one of the holiest places for Hindus. In Sanskrit, Har means Shiva, Hari means Vishnu, and Dwar means gate. Haridwar is therefore the gateway to the two holy shrines of Shiva and Vishnu. Shiva is the destroyer of evil, and Vishnu is the protector of life. Together, these two sacred energies abolish evil and restore order in our lives and in the world. Here there is balance. The rivers of the Ganges join together. While we met in this divine place, our stories connected *through* this writing process. Our singular voices started to harmonize in this clarion call to reclaim and reimagine education.

Together, we practiced rituals of awakening, encountered the power of magnetic pedagogy, and strived to integrate the lessons into a living justice.

From our experience, this process embodies a slowing down that is antithetical to many of our daily lives and demands. We realize that you are busy and probably, like us, too often multitasking and in a rush. We're so used to gathering information quickly—consider how fast you run through emails or grab excerpts from an article. While this allows us to move fast, it inhibits a level of integration into our daily lives. For this reason, the pages before you have been written with a slower rhythm in mind. Allow yourself to pause; we actually encourage it. As our beloved reader, please listen carefully and insert yourself into the stories, poems, and parables. This is a guided meditation and is meant to be experienced.

> *Encounters with mentors and subjects*
> *can awaken a sense of self and yield clues to who we are.*
> *But the call to teach does not come from external encounters alone—no outward*
> *teacher or teaching will have much effect until my soul assents.*
> *Any authentic call ultimately comes from the voice of the teacher within,*
> *the voice that invites me to honor the nature of my true self.*
> ~ Parker Palmer ~

Let the journey begin.

Notes

1. P. Yogananda. (1982). *Metaphysical Meditations*. Los Angeles: Self-Realization Fellowship, p. 53.
2. D. Orr. (1994). *Earth in Mind: On Education, Environment, and the Human Prospect*. Washington, DC: Island Press, p. 12.
3. For more information on Dev Sanskriti Vishwavidyalaya, visit: www.dsvv.ac.in/dev-sanskriti-university/.
4. Dhikr (or zikr) is an Arabic word meaning "remembrance." It is a rhythmic repetition of ritual prayer practiced by Muslim mystics (Sufis) for the purpose of glorifying God and achieving spiritual realization and unification.
5. Toni Morrison. www.youtube.com/watch?v=6S7zGgL6Suw.
6. This concept arose from a conversation with my colleague Dr. Sheeva Sabati, who studies the intersections of ethics and decolonization.

1
MEDITATION ON EDUCATION

What would an education of the soul look like?
~ Kabir ~

The Soul of Learning presents a lens on teaching and learning that weaves together our respective backgrounds of contemplative and critical pedagogies with perennial wisdom. Throughout these pages, we have constructed a path for you, our reader, to experience education as a living discipline. An education that is so deeply infused with soul that the results are imbued with authenticity, wisdom, compassion, and living justice. For it is the soul that grants these gifts and guides us to lead an awakened, authentic, compassionate, and harmonious life.

Along this journey, we can hear the words of Ella Baker as she tells us, "The system under which we now exist has to be radically changed. This means that we are going to have to learn to think in radical terms." To accomplish Baker's vision, we need to do the internal work that will allow us to reconnect and rediscover the essence and roots of our humanity. We yearn for drastic changes in society and in our selves. We also believe the time is now. Right now. *This* particular moment is spectacular. "The pandemic is a portal," Arundhati Roy (2020) explains: "Historically, pandemics have forced humans to break with the past and imagine their world anew. This one is no different. It is a portal, a gateway between one world and the next." Thus, we are at a crossroads: one path leads forward toward transformation and the other a return to the status quo. May we not return to "normal."

The Soul of Learning is our small attempt to bring us through the portal. Our intentions are simple. There is no learning without soul. An education about the soul is spiritual in nature. While many of the readings may seem religious, per se, they are part of the greater opus of the world's literature and can be experienced as "living revelations." Inside these pages, we enter into sacred dialogue with parables and poets spanning across time and cultures. Through a carefully curated selection of these literary pieces and activities, we embark on various *rituals of awakening*. This generative process is meant to challenge and inspire you to come face to face with yourself and each other as a form of pedagogical disruption. Altogether our method is meant to be transformative, offering contemplative and innovative ways to read, teach, learn, lead, and live.

May these words reach your heart, reflect your purpose, and enliven the world.

Every being with a gift,
Every being with a responsibility.
~ Robin Kimmerer[1] ~

As a first step, we want to personally welcome you into this experience of the interior and the infinite. Please accept our invitation and make yourself feel at home. Take a deep breath—and let it fill you from the soles of your feet all the way through to the crown upon your head—and allow yourself to relax into the moment. Lay your burdens down. Trust yourself, your intuition. Just pause and be.

Breathe...Breathe...Breathe.

In 1968, Thomas Merton discussed the "innate violence" of being too busy with the "rush and pressure of modern life" (p. 81). Jane Dalton (2018) extended this idea when she writes, "Ignoring my body and my heart, I force personal will to complete my 'to do' tasks, despite signs of fatigue or stress. I become oriented toward goals and making things happen, pushing against the very loud messages I receive to pause" (p. 21). Moving from the personal to the political, Leigh Patel (2016) connects slowing down to decolonial practices, consciously reorienting oneself in relation to space and time. She writes, "Pausing is useful, even necessary, particularly in these modern times in which colonial projects have shaped technology, knowledge, and connection to be a veritable nonstop stimulations of tweets, status updates, and deadlines, all competing for our attention" (p. 1). Pausing can actually be a productive interruption to competitive ways of *doing*. When we pause, we can shift into our human *being*.

People, just like plants and animals, have a purpose. The sacred pause can help us discover our inner compass.

Seek That

There is a fire within you that gives you life—
Seek that.
In your body is a precious jewel—
Seek that.
Oh, wandering Sufi,
If you are in search of the greatest treasure,
Don't look outside,
Look within, and seek That.
~ Rumi ~

When we are seeking our truest self, we often start this journey of awakening—alone. However, that's not the complete truth. We have within us the past and future, ancestors and descendants. Our lives merely and magnificently a bridge between yesterday and tomorrow. Right now, we have before us the most precious present. We are grateful for this moment and these words. This page and your attention. We are actually here in this moment—together.

How beautiful it is to come together for the purpose of learning. Consider teaching as a ritual, a ceremony. In Latin, *caerimonia* means *holy* and *sacred*; it is holistic and whole-making, both grounding and elevating. As Robin Kimmerer (2013) shares in *Braiding Sweetgrass*, "Ceremony focuses attention so that attention becomes intention . . . These are ceremonies that magnify life" (p. 249). This magnetism is enlightening and regenerative, a creative force that moves us from objects to subjects, from passive to powerful.

Any place we gather becomes a ceremony on the way.
~ Rumi ~

As a form of ceremony, how do we hold one another and ourselves to higher states of being and deeper ways of living in and with each other? Helminski (2017), provides an answer:

> A seed has no energy of its own, but it can respond in the right environment. Every form of life has a capacity for response but none so much as the human being. . . . The cultivation we need to provide is through conscious awareness. This makes the difference between nominally being alive and being alive abundantly (p. 14).

As we pivot toward conscious awareness, we start to see ourselves with greater clarity. This form of honesty can be hard and painful. It requires accountability, integrity, and responsibility. Any commitment to change takes work and discipline guided by wisdom, beauty, and grace.

As human beings, we have the incredible capacity to change and be changed. Learning—in its most liberating state—allows us to let go of preconceived notions, stretch our ideas, expand our consciousness, and cultivate understanding. Moving from the known into the unknown can be terrifying, but as Morrison (1998) explains: "What you do know is that you are human and therefore educable, and therefore capable of learning how to learn" (p. 141). Leigh Patel (2016) extends this conversation when she writes, "Learning is fundamentally a fugitive, transformative act. It runs from what was previously known, to become something not yet known" (p. 6).

What will come of this transformative work? Who are you now? Who will you become? As authors of this text, we do not hold the answers, but we are intent on inspiring you, challenging you, shapeshifting perspectives, and impacting the landscape of learning.

Our book builds upon the long legacy of freedom dreams, contemplative thinkers, and contemporary abolitionists (Kelley, 2002; Love, 2019; Palmer, 1993, 2004). We are inspired by Tuck and Yang (2018), who describe being born under the rising sign of social justice. What we are offering is a journey as a way to tap into new possibilities for teaching, learning, and living. Building on this theme, we wonder, like Keno Evol (2020) in *A Garden of Black Joy*, "What if we began at a kind of unachievability? What if we began there and still proceeded? Not because we'll win but because we'll have an experience within our activities. Because we'll get closer to each other" (p. 4). As we get closer to each other, Jarrett (2021) urges us to consider, "What does a relationship look like when freedom and integrity are the highest shared priorities and love is merely a reflection of those commitments" (p. 307)?

The Soul of Learning is an invitation to pursue our purpose as teachers, mentors, and students. It's a challenge for radical vulnerability, authentic openings, and critical hope. Hope, like faith, is a beautiful tool of resistance in a system that can often stifle the soul.

As the authors of this text, we want to bring the sacred into schooling. But to do so, we have to tease apart the differences between teaching as profession and teaching as transgression (hooks, 1994); between the institution of schooling and the nature of learning; between oppression and liberation.

> *A teacher who is not free to teach is not a teacher . . . to teach, is a revolutionary act.*
> ~ James Baldwin[2] ~

While Baldwin defines teaching as emancipatory, this is not the way most teachers define our profession. Nor does it encompass our training.

Far too often, schools are tools of the state. Teachers merely cogs in the machinery of indoctrination and assimilation. This is sad but all too accurate. Colonial-based school systems continue to *test what students know* but often disregard *how they grow*. This is not just a current crisis.

Generations of scholars have examined the ideological tensions surrounding public schooling—from theories of social reproduction to ones of social resistance (Adams, 1995; Apple, 1995; Bourdieu, Passeron & Nice, 1977; Bowles & Gintis, 1976; Freire, 1970; MacLeod, 1995; Oakes, 1985; Noguera, 2003; Watson, 2018; Woodson, 1933). And many schools—as machines of patriarchy, white supremacy, and capitalist pursuits—are structures of inequality and disproportionality. Wedded to coloniality, industrialism, and materialism. But this is not the true function of education! There are times throughout history when schools have served as centers of transformative community practice (Bache, 2008; Gunnlaugson, Scott, Bai & Sarath, 2019; Keator, 2018; Lichtmann, 2005; Miller, 2000; Givens, 2021; Payne & Strickland, 2008; Watson, 2012). Evident tensions surrounding the purpose of school persist. These debates have waged on for far too long. Is schooling in its current state working? No. We need a new compass and a new road map to find our way home.

The master's tools will never dismantle the master's house.
~ Audre Lorde ~

Harkening back to the words of W.E.B. DuBois in 1903, he taught us that "Education must *not* simply *teach work*, it must *teach life*."[3] So, then, what if the purpose of school is the learning of life itself? How would this change our orientation and direction?

For millennia, there have been amazing teachers guiding humanity. These educators wrote about another way of living. "Go inward," they whisper through the portal, "go inward." Alexis Grumbs (2020) continues, "I do commit to the work of going deep enough to find the necessary food that lights us up inside. I love you, and I have so much to learn. . . . I love you, and how generous—how downright miraculous—it is that life would let me learn like this" (p. 57).

From this perspective, the purpose of education is not only "to teach life," as noted by DuBois. It is to thrive; it is to magnify life itself. Learning, like love, is accessible to all. And education happens everywhere where love abounds.

The greatest classroom dwells within the heart. *Pause on that.* The classroom of all classrooms exists within. Therefore, we need to develop an intimate relationship with our heart and soul. Lichtmann (2005) points out: "If teaching and learning reach the stage of the heart, they become truly contemplative and integrative because only heart can meditate between the body and the mind. Only the heart can bring together the sense perceptions of attention and the cognitive energies of reflection" (p. 97).

This is not education as a noun. It is education as verb. We want to use this opportunity to connect to ancient traditions of awakening. In *The Alchemist* (1998), Paulo Coelho writes about this eternal energy that connects us to our divine existence:

> When you want something with all your heart, that's when you are closest to the Soul of the World. It's always a positive force. . . . Everything on earth is being continuously transformed, because the earth is alive . . . and it is part of that soul. We are part of that soul (pp. 78–79).

For far too long, the school system has drained and depleted the life energy of teachers and students. This busyness leaves little to no room for our inner being to emerge. There's so little time to reflect. This is a main issue, because it is through contemplation that the soul comes to grow, learn, and know. In *Education and the Soul*, Miller (2000) notes, "We are taught to find the right answer or develop the right argument. By ignoring or denying contemplation the soul is also denied. The soul hides away while our minds analyze, memorize and categorize" (p. 29).

6 Meditation on Education

It is time to re-position the soul at the center of pedagogy and community. Without soul, there is no life, no power, no light and therefore no repairing, renaissance, or regeneration. In other words, when we are not living in alignment with our soul, we're like a tree without roots. No roots, no nourishment. We need to be radical and reclaim the roots of learning.

Education, as a sacred science and divine discipline, has existed long before the traditional schoolhouse. This is important to recognize. "The connections made by good teachers," explains Palmer (2007), "are held not in their methods but in their hearts—meaning heart in its ancient sense, the place where intellect and emotion and spirit and will converge in the human self" (p. 11). Thus, the harmony of holistic healing and learning becomes an intersection. A location. A place where the heart's deep gladness meets the world's deep hunger.[4]

As Grace Lee Boggs points out, "If we could work intergenerationally as solutionaries to all the challenges to our well-being and existence that would be all the school we need."[5] This kind of work is intersubjective, dialogic, and revolutionary. It compels us to confront ourselves—in, with, and through communion with others. Consciousness expands our connectivity; the whole is greater than what any individual holds alone.

Awaken the Inner Teacher

Take off the teacher hat.
The scholar credentials,
The ego and accolades.
We grow,
in silence.
We transform within the darkness of Mother Earth.
Breath by breath,
heartbeat by heartbeat.
In the solitude and silence.
Alone-ness inside that magnificent womb of
Gaia.
We are on an inward journey
to understand who we are,
our deeper purpose in life
Seed in the ground.
Dying, opening, sprouting, growing, blossoming.
~ Mary Keator ~

The Soul of Learning takes the notion of theory-to-practice into another domain—an important leap inward through the portal of our educational possibilities. As our pedagogy aligns art, science, and soul, we're able to manifest new educational ecosystems of sacred transformation.

While this book is directed toward teachers, in the broadest sense, we realize that all people are students on a divine path of self-discovery called life. Whether you're from privilege or poverty, surrounded by serenity or sirens, our learning starts within.

> *I wonder, I wonder if you really knew, that I see God in you.*
> ~ India Arie ~

Whoever you are: *please know that we need you on this journey!* Wherever you are: *welcome!* We are here to reconnect with the knowledge of the saints and sages, prophets, and poets. These soul surgeons provide us with tools to break open and get free. This is a litany of liberation, a human soliloquy of potentiality. Our hope is that through this meditative reading practice, you'll awaken to learning as a sacred act in direct relationship with the divine text of your life.

We aspire to accompany and guide you toward the beauty, wisdom, truth, and justice of your inner light. To support this process, we've laid steppingstones and lit candles as you make your way toward new realizations, integration, and wholeness. An offering toward holistic re-membering. We've done our best to craft a roadmap that is inspiring and useful and that will perhaps even excite the traveler. Like any great adventure, there is a hidden treasure. But for us, the key that unlocks this treasure is found within.

The ultimate goal of this awakening is your sovereignty. True sovereignty aligns your innate potential and magnifies your natural, healthy magnetic frequency. You literally and figuratively become a positive force not just for yourself but in the world. May you come to experience collective belonging and arrive in beloved community.

To begin, below are some teachers of awakening. Each offers a particular orientation to learning and life, steps into educational meditations. *What do you hear them sharing about our divine purpose?*

True Work

Human beings come into this world
to do particular work.
That work is their purpose,
and each is specific to the person.
If you forget everything else and not this,
there's nothing to worry about.
If you remember everything else and
forget your true work,
then you will have done nothing in your life.

~ Rumi

8 Meditation on Education

The Kingdom of God

Jesus was asked, "When will the Kingdom of God come?"
He answered, "The coming of the Kingdom of God cannot be observed.
People will not say, 'Look! Here it is! Or 'Look! There it is!
For the Kingdom of God is within you."

~ The Gospel of Luke

The Summer Day

Who made the world?
Who made the swan, and the black bear?
Who made the grasshopper?
This grasshopper, I mean—
the one who has flung herself out of the grass,
the one who is eating sugar out of my hand,
who is moving her jaws back and forth instead of up and down—
who is gazing around with her enormous and complicated eyes.
Now she lifts her pale forearms and thoroughly washes her face.
Now she snaps her wings open, and floats away.
I don't know exactly what a prayer is.
I do know how to pay attention, how to fall down
into the grass, how to kneel in the grass,
how to be idle and blessed, how to stroll through the fields,
which is what I have been doing all day.
Tell me, what else should I have done?
Doesn't everything die at last, and too soon?
Tell me, what is it you plan to do
With your one wild and precious life?

~ Mary Oliver

What a Time to Be Alive.

Each day a blessing and burden
Daily call and responsibility
A joy and a duty to celebrate and fight
with every last breath
for those who had theirs
taken from them

I turned 36 yesterday

For Jewish folks, multiples of 18 are holy
18 means Chai means Life
So if I turn 36, is this my second life?

Or my third?
How do we celebrate life amidst its opposite?
Pandemic and police
Twin viruses
Killing with impunity
What do I tell my sons in the morning?
Do we light candles for cakes or vigils?
Prayers or protests?
I don't speak Hebrew
but all I want for my birthday this year
is from my lips to God's ears
Fuck the Police
I shout to the moon
as I turn another revolution of the sun
I am the son of fighters
The father of laughers
The lover of a healer
I am one year older in a country
Searching for new life
Breaking free of white lies
And white tears and white fascists
The virus is here
But so are we
I am so grateful
to be here with you
What a time to be alive.
~ Josh Healey, June 2020

Fear

It is said that before entering the sea
a river trembles with fear.
She looks back at the path she has traveled,
from the peaks of the mountains,
the long winding road crossing forests and villages.
And in front of her,
she sees an ocean so vast,
that to enter
there seems nothing more than to disappear forever.
But there is no other way.
The river cannot go back.
Nobody can go back.
To go back is impossible in existence.

> The river needs to take the risk
> of entering the ocean
> because only then will fear disappear,
> because that's where the river will know
> it's not about disappearing into the ocean,
> but of becoming the ocean.
>
> ~ Khalil Gibran

Although these mystics and poets span many miles and a myriad of years, they have each tapped into a secret. As we are, we are not fully awake. As Mary's teacher Shyam shared, "We are lost in a dream. Wake up and love with laughter!" Often, we seek life in all the wrong places, looking into manufactured spaces rather than into the natural world. The time to wake up is here. Go in, they urge, and seek that which gives life joy and purpose. Go in and discover the mystery of who you are and why you are here. Wow, what a wonderful time to be alive!

As a closing activity to this chapter, call into your mind someone that teaches, grounds, centers, and/or brings you peace. Visualize this person. What is the name of this shero or hero?

The name of one of my most inspiring teachers: _____.

Say their name. Be bold and loud and loving. Full of a heart beating. Tap into the rhythm and energy that surrounds you. Yes, we are regaining our foothold and reclaiming education's sacred power. Are you ready? Join us as we take steps forward one deep breath at a time.

Notes

1. R. Kimmerer. (2013). *Braiding Sweetgrass: Indigenous Wisdom, Scientific Knowledge, and the Teachings of Plants.* Minneapolis, MN: Milkweed, p. 211.
2. J. Baldwin. (1973). *A Dialogue: James Baldwin and Nikki Giovanni.* Philadelphia: Lippincott, pp. 74–75.
3. *From* W. E. B. DuBois. (1903). "The Talented Tenth." In *The Negro Problem: A Series of Articles by Representative American Negroes of Today.* New York: James Pott, pp. 33–75.
4. Adapted from Frederick Buechner, who is an American writer, novelist, poet, autobiographer, essayist, preacher, and theologian.
5. Scholar activist, G. L. Boggs. (2007). *Opening Ceremony at the Allied Media Conference in Detroit Michigan.* https://amc.alliedmedia.org/.

2
SILENCE

The eternal Word itself is silent beyond silence.
~ Jean-Yves Leloup[1] ~

Silence is not simply the cessation from an overactive life; it is a state of being in which we settle into a sacred space of timelessness. Silence is the language of the soul, *still small voice* the speaking from deep within our hearts, calling us to deepen our self-awareness and integrate it into our lives in authentic and meaningful ways. Yet, in reality, the sheer busyness of our lives distracts us from journeying deeper into the silent moments. However, silence is all around us. It is found between activities and even between breaths.

Think about the rhythms that define your days and nights.

For many, a typical day begins with waking up and reaching for our phones. Throughout the day, we tend to juggle email, social media, and Zoom calls while also maintaining the basic necessities of life. Notice how these activities and demands of daily life involve us doing something. Guided by task lists, agendas, and calendars, we feel a sense of accomplishment when we're able to check off items off *that* task list. Amid the busyness of these responsibilities, we might go for a walk, hang with loved ones, or binge watch a Netflix series. We're constantly seeking ways to replenish, but is it working? Although each of these encounters arising in the outer world of our lives has purpose and meaning, this noise—even joyful, sacred sounds—can veil the power of silence.

Think about the times you ignored the invitation to dwell in the silence of your heart and answer the call to create time for reflection, introspection, and contemplation.

> *There is a way between voice and presence,*
> *where information flows.*
> *In disciplined silence it opens;*
> *with wandering talk it closes.*
> ~ Rumi ~

Where is your silence?
    When do you sit still and take a pause?
        Is your rhythm offbeat with the Uni-verse?
            Is your way of working meaningless, uninspiring, and discouraging?

These questions can reorientate all of us onto a different path and lead us toward new answers and deeper meaning.

Notice, as we begin to ponder stillness, silence emerges. When we intentionally prioritize time to dwell in silence, we learn to let go of *doing* and embrace *being*. This self-realization is the starting point and the initial step to understanding justice as living in right relationship with authentic self and one another. Although at times this can feel challenging and unsettling, our commitment to a *praxis of silence* reveals our true nature.

> *Is stillness just the absence of noise and content?*
> *No, it is intelligence itself—the underlying consciousness*
> *out of which every form is born.*
> ~ Eckhart Tolle ~

Inside your daily life, where are the truly silent moments? Those moments that allow you to submerge yourself into the deep inner stillness, beyond the noise and content, to connect with what Tolle (2003) refers to as the "underlying consciousness out of which every form is born" (p. 7). Yes, in and through silence, we too can connect with one another. This source of life nourishes and enlightens the body, mind, and heart. A place of purposeful expansion and endless potentialities—like a well that never runs dry.

Silence is a sacred doorway that can lead us on an inward path in search of truth and wisdom, love, and compassion. At first, to be still reveals to us our inner noise. We begin to notice the incessant interior chatter of the mind, the restlessness of the body, and the longing inside the heart. Remain steadfast. Inside the stillness, we enter the dark void and creative tension of silence.

Wherever we live on earth, we can peer upward into the night sky and feel its silent majesty. Go out at night and look in between the stars. It is this vast open space that holds our existence. According to quantum physics, the vastness that we see in the night sky mirrors the vastness within ourselves and our cells.

*As above, so below,
as within, so without,
as the universe, so the soul.*
~ Hermes Trismegistus ~

But where is the silence within? Unlike the silence of the night sky, our interior world is not so still. Our internal waters (which make up approximately 70% of our body) often hide the stillness. Loud and turbulent thoughts crash like waves inside us, the undertow pulling us deeper into the turmoil.

At times, we can feel like we're drowning.

All too often, we get caught in these thought waves, but there is another option. We can watch and observe them; let them rise and fall like the tide. Staying with the ocean metaphor, we have the capacity to quiet the waters within and enter the peaceful abyss. We all have the innate ability for stillness. Bruce Lee proclaimed, "Be water, my friend." If we achieve stillness, the water becomes a calm, sacred mirror. We begin to see ourselves more clearly.

*"Men [and Women] do not mirror themselves in running water—
they mirror themselves in still water."*
~ Zhuangzi ~

Silence is a tool of perception and revelation. The quiet moments reflect back to us our soul's longing and our heart's deepest desires. As we embrace the silence, thoughts and feelings will continue to arise. Instead of fighting them, we can witness them. So, let each emotion emerge, acknowledge it, and let it leave. By doing this practice, the mind will slow down. These quiet waters become the mirror of alignment, transforming us into a living vessel. We become attune to the rhythm of the universe and its pulsating dance between silence and sound.

*Like water which can clearly mirror the sky and the trees
only so long as its surface is undisturbed,
the mind can only reflect the true image of the Self
when it is tranquil and wholly relaxed.*
~ Indra Devi ~

As we learn to embody the power of silence, we will be able to nourish this silent space throughout our lives. Silence no longer becomes uncomfortable. Rather, we discover its actual purpose and power.

Consciously make an effort to befriend silence: *Set a one-minute timer and just sit still. Allow yourself to get very quiet. Lean into its emptiness.* Once you feel comfortable with one minute, gradually increase the time, allowing stillness and silence to become a part of your routine.

Silence is an unknown abyss where there are no questions or answers, no prescribed agenda. Silence is part of our humanity.

> *Schools need to stop blaming and punishing*
> *children for being human.*
> ~ Steven Wolk[2] ~

Imagine the visceral noisiness of school. Bells ringing. Teachers talking. Students talking. The rush between classes. Educators are trained to fill each and every minute with instruction. Healthy silence isn't valued and definitely not encouraged.

Productive silence is natural. It is intentional, generative, and explorative. Imagine teachers and students engaged in learning through silence. Whereas *destructive silence* is forced. It is exploitive, demeaning, and controlling; teachers and administrators forcing students to be quiet. Unfortunately, the latter dominates schools today.

Schooling has become overly mechanical and draconian; it has lost its organic purpose. Classrooms are filled with lectures, duties and deadlines. Whether we're in the university or K-12 setting, there are entrapments that stifle learning. When used pedagogically, silence is an incredible teaching tool that can help decrease anxiety and propel inner peace. Turning toward the work of John Miller (2000) in *Education and the Soul*, he explains:

Our culture is drowning in sound bites and chatter. The more talk, the less we hear:

> Our education system has too little respect for silence. In silence, we can learn to listen . . . we can begin to hear other people at a much deeper level. . . . By honoring silence and space, we begin to bring some sort of balance to our culture and our lives (p. 136).

When we, as educators, provide students with quiet space, we honor and engage their whole being. As Lichtmann (2005) notes, "Silence, can create hospitality, though it may bring awkwardness in the door with it. When we invite silence into the learning space, we send a signal that we want our students to reach for their authentic selves, not just to impress or please us" (p. 99).

How can we begin to cultivate silence within ourselves? How do we create inner boundaries to stay still in the silence even though we are constantly overcome with thoughts and feelings?

Consider that we could begin class with a moment of silence. Or perhaps, we create space between the words that we're reading, for instance, reading slowing and ritualistically so that each word, sound, and pause encapsulates the rendering of a text. Another point to consider is the use of time itself. For example, we can give ample opportunities for students to reflect quietly without an action, encouraging students to sit and settle into the silence before responding on paper or even talking out loud.

As a teaching tool, intentional, quiet moments nurture growth and nourish intellectual awakening. Silence takes us into the seeds of our pain, power, and possibilities. How do we guide students to listen to the silence instead of being overtaken by their thoughts and feelings? What are we quietly and intentionally growing inside our classroom and ourselves?

We encourage you to encounter the challenging inner terrain, commit to the journey, and move through it toward greater clarity. This is not easy, and it demands various acts of personal courage. Silence can feel uncomfortable, even disturbing and disarming. However, this angst can actually help us emerge. Discomfort is an essential part of growth, and often we struggle with accepting it. However, when we surrender into the process, we are able to till the soil, plant our seeds, break open in tenderness, and slowly grow and transform. The result is a regenerative garden that helps us reach a fuller potential.

Next, we present some teachers of silence. These lessons cross time and continents, yet there are distinct commonalities. Take the time to read and re-read these pieces out loud and silently. As you read, remember to allow space for the silence between the words and between the verses. *What is being revealed about silence? What is the essential lesson? What is your relationship with silence?*

The Cricket Story

Once two friends were walking down the sidewalk on a busy street during rush hour. There were all sorts of noise in the city—car horns honking, feet shuffling, people talking! And amid all the noise, one of the friends turned to the other and said, "I hear a cricket."

"No way," her friend responded. "How could you hear a cricket with all of this noise? You must be imagining it. Besides, I've never seen a cricket in the city."

"No, really, I do hear a cricket. I'll show you." She stopped for a moment, then led her friend across the street to a big cement planter with a tree in it. Pushing back the leaves, she found a little brown cricket.

"That's amazing!" said her friend, "You must have a super-human hearing. What's your secret?"

"No, my hearing is just the same as yours. There's no secret," the first woman replied. "Watch; I'll show you." She reached into her pocket, pulled out some loose change, and threw it on the sidewalk. Amid all of the noise of the city, everyone within 30 feet turned their head to see where the sound of the money was coming from.

"See?" she said. "It's all a matter of what you are listening for."

Silence is not the absence of noise but the refined tuning of the soul to the sounds and movements that usually go unnoticed.

~ Elisa Davy Pearmain

! Rumi's Silence

Rumi wrote much about silence.
Does that seem strange?

Poets live with silence:
the silence before the poem;
the silence whence the poem comes;

the silence in between the words, as you
drink the words, watch them glide through your mind,
feel them slide down your throat

towards your heart;

the silence which you share with the poet
when the poem ends, sitting side by side,
feeling one another being one heart;

the silence after the poem,
when you are a different person
from the person who started reading the poem,
think differently, move differently,

act differently; know Rumi a little better
as a friend; know yourself a little more
as a friend.

Rumi was asked, why do you
talk, talk, talk, so much
about silence?

He said, the radiant one inside me
has said nothing.

And that's the silence which we listen to
and hear in Rumi's heart,
here, sitting in the cool shade
which the scent of roses seems to love,
while the fountain gently plays like a poet
with sound and silence.

~ Michael Shepherd

In the Depths of Solitude: Dedicated 2 Me

I exist in the depths of solitude
pondering my true goal
Trying 2 find peace of mind
and still preserve my soul
CONSTANTLY yearning 2 be accepted
and from all receive respect
Never compromising but sometimes risky
and that is my only regret
A young heart with an old soul
how can there be peace
How can I be in the depth of solitude
when there R 2 inside of me
This Duo within me causes
the perfect opportunity
2 learn and live twice as fast
as those who accept simplicity

~ Tupac Amaru Shakur

In Silence

A guide has entered this life in silence.
His message is only heard in silence.

Take a sip of his precious wine and lose yourself.
Don't insult the greatness of his love,
For he helps all those who suffer in silence.
Polish the mirror between the breaths.
Go with him, beyond words.
He knows your every deed.
He is the one who moves the wheel of heaven, in silence.
Every thought is buried in your heart;
He will reveal them one by one, in silence.

Turn each of your thoughts into a bird
And let them fly to the other world.
One is an owl, one is a falcon, one is a crow.
Each one is different from the others
But they are all the same in silence.

To see the Moon that cannot be seen
Turn your eyes inward
And look at yourself, in silence.

~ Rumi

18 Silence

> *Psalm 46:10*
>
> Be still and know that I am God

———

Each of the writers in these texts enter into silence from different eras and locations. Michael Shepherd asks why Rumi talks so much about silence, and Tupac asks himself the question: "How can there be peace/how can I be in the depth of solitude when there R 2 inside of me?" These layers of introspection are helpful and provide glimpses into this universal yearning for a personal sanctuary that exists within our most authentic selves.

Some essential lessons to consider:

- Silence is timeless and universal.
- Even amid the noises of life, silence remains within us.
- We always have access to internal silence.
- Silence is not a waste of time; it is a place of divine possibility.
- Silence exists before words, after words, and between words and worlds.

Personal activity:

- Set your alarm for four minutes. During these four minutes, be still and surrender into the silence.
- *Lectio Divina* is a contemplative method of reading, reflecting, and responding to texts. Select a word or verse (from the collections in this chapter) that inspired or challenged you and write it down. Slowly read this word or verse a few times to yourself while carefully considering it. What do you hear? How are these words speaking to you in the midst of your life today?

_____
_____
_____
_____
_____
_____
_____

Collective practices:

Classrooms are fertile ground to co-create organic generative experiences that cultivate personal mastery and collective responsibility. As we are digesting these lessons on silence, it's critical that we are active participants and not just recipients of the information.

As teachers of sacred space, there are number of ways to utilize these lessons on silence in multiple learning contexts.

For example, building on the earlier personal activity, invite students to share in small groups or with the whole class their word or verse along with why it spoke to them. As another activity, take a moment to play a song and concentrate on the silent moments between the notes and within the silence inside the rhythm.

An additional, opening activity is to ask students to draw what silence looks and/or feels like. What are their intuitive perceptions? After doing this exercise, exchange the art pieces. Share each student's art ritualistically—silently at first and then out loud.

Ask the group to sit in silence. Use a sound (like a chime) to demarcate the time—even if it's just a couple of minutes. Take a break and make some noise. And then sit again in the silence; this time try for a bit longer. After this routine (and building on Rumi's stanza), ask them *what recurring messages do you hear inside your silence?*

- _____
- _____
- _____

We are the divine text. Essentially, our heart is the Kaaba, our bodies the Ark of the Covenant. Mystical lessons and sacred books are not finite; rather, they are an invitation to explore infinity.

May we surrender to silence in order to hear our living breath breathing.

Your teacher can open the door,
but you must enter by yourself.
~ Chinese Proverb ~

Notes

1. J. Y. Leloup. (2003). *Being Still: Reflections on an Ancient Mystical Tradition.* Mahwah, NJ: Paulist Press, p. 89.
2. S. Wolk. (1998). *A Democratic Classroom.* Portsmouth, NH: Heinemann Press, p. 22.

3
JUST BREATHE

Who am I in the midst of all this thought traffic?
~ Rumi ~

Within the pages of this chapter, we will engage in self-inquiry. Like Rumi, we, too, recognize the traffic jam of thoughts. One after another speeding through the mind. Never slowing, never stopping. Each outpacing the other along an endless information speedway, round and round, never really going anywhere.

Are you exhausted?

Let's take a break from all this traffic and imagine the ocean. How does this sound? Picture the waves. Notice them form and build. Some roll in gently, while others rush forcefully and turbulently to the shore. These waves, like our thoughts, distract us from seeing clearly below the surface. Who am I, in the midst of these thought waves, constantly arising? Inhale, exhale. Breathe. Slow and conscious. Notice the thought waves quiet with each breath, the mind clears, and below the surface, the Self rests peaceful, conscious and undisturbed.

Stress suffocates our breathing, almost like a chokehold. Do we even have the energy, time, and space to take a full breath repeatedly throughout the day? Linda Stone, a former Apple and Microsoft executive, has written about what she calls "email apnea," pointing to our tendency to hold our breath while doing email."[1] Consider just how many breaths we may be holding throughout the day. The quality of our breathing not only reflects our state of mind but also affects it.

Let's cultivate a relationship with our breath: *Fill your temple with a slow deep breath. Experience the power of a full inhalation—down into the base of your spine. Then take a long, slow exhalation.*

All life breathes. We are born through the breath. And when we die, our breath dissolves into the cosmic breath. Wow, give thanks for the breath!

DOI: 10.4324/9781003197164-3

Consider that for a plant to grow, it needs various nourishment such as good soil, water, air, and sunlight, and some, such as a tomato plant or bean plant, need support. Yet there are plants that can also survive in the most grueling environments, even with minimal amounts of soil, water, and moisture. Even under these conditions, plants still need to breathe. Like any living thing, plants survive through respiration, inhaling carbon dioxide and exhaling oxygen.

In the previous chapter, we concentrated on silence, the sky, and water. The most abundant source of oxygen on Earth is water (H_2O), a molecule that contains two hydrogen atoms and one oxygen atom. Water is life, just as breath is life. Yet we are not just abstract forms of water and breath. As material, physical, and organic beings like trees and birds, we are in a symbiotic and synergistic relationship with the living world. In *Atmospheres of Breathing*, John Peters (2018) explains our collective and cooperative respiration cycle:

> Respiration, which produces carbon dioxide and water while burning sugars by means of oxygen, is the counterpart of photosynthesis, the transformation of light energy into chemical energy. When we breathe in, we unravel the work done by some plant remote in time and space. Respiration is the consumption of energy, photosynthesis its storage. Breathing is thus connected to the total circulation of life on our planet (p. 183).

To tap into this ecosystem takes breath because, like we mentioned before, all life breathes.

When we root ourselves to our own bodies, we can become like the plant, or as Tupac recites in the forthcoming passage, the rose that grows from the cracks in the concrete. Let's go inside ourselves, find the opening, and fill our bodies with oxygen.

The Rose That Grew from Concrete

Did u hear about the rose that grew from a crack
In the concrete
Proving nature's laws wrong it learned 2 walk
Without having feet
Funny it seems but by keeping its dreams
It learned 2 breathe fresh air
Long live the rose that grew from concrete
When no one else cared!
~ Tupac Amaru Shakur ~

In "The Possibility of a New Respiratory Ontology," Berndtson (Škof & Berndtson, 2018) illuminates the teachings of Japanese Aikido Master Shinichi, who shares that "nothing is more important than breathing, breathing, breathing." By practicing regularly, you enter a "world of nothing but breathing. You will feel as if it is the universal, not yourself, who is doing the breathing" (p. 29).

Ah, the breath. The key to life. Breath nourishes us and breathes us into existence moment to moment, day to day.

> *My breath is prayer, the shape of life, evolving name.*
> *All I can see is just the blur that says life moves.*
> *I stay in prayer, and reach to listen for your breath.*
> ~ Alexis Pauline Gumbs[2] ~

Have you ever considered that we all share this one breath together? Reflect on this. All of us are breathing the same one breath that is re-inspired and re-generated again and again. The entire earth is breathing! As a prime example, our exhalation becomes the plants' inhalation, and the plants' exhalation becomes our inhalation. The world is breathing as One. As we connect to the universal breath, our universe expands.

> *All things share the same breath*
> *the beast, the tree, the [woman] man . . .*
> *The air shares its spirit with all the life it supports.*
> ~ Chief Seattle[3] ~

As we experience the universal nature of breathing, something begins to shift. Take a moment to settle into this interconnected reality. Practice breathing with the world. Begin to notice that the rhythm of the breath is often swift, short, and shallow. Yet with each intentional breath, it becomes more expansive, generous, and generative. We are opening ourselves.

To breathe deeply is to trust. First, we have to learn to empty the breath—with a full exhalation—before we can receive a new breath of inhalation. We exhale what we think we know. *Release.* We inhale the new moment. *Exist.*

As we journey deeper into the breath, the outer world gently fades away, revealing the inner clamor, chaos, and confusion that's running rampant through our minds. Quieting our exterior world discloses our inner reality, its disarray. What is the process of emptying our mental thoughts? And why is it important? To help answer these questions, let's dive into an ancient Zen story.

In *The Empty Cup*, a scholar comes to visit a Zen Master. Instead of being calm and open in the Master's presence, his driving eagerness to convey his ideas became his main impediment:

> One day the Zen Master Nan-in had a visit from a foreign scholar of Eastern religions who came to inquire about Zen. Instead of listening to the

Master, however, the visitor kept talking on and on about his own ideas and all that he knew.

After awhile of this talking, Nan-in served tea. He poured the tea into his visitor's cup until it was full, and then he kept on pouring. The tea poured over the side of the cup, filled the saucer, and then spilled over onto the man's pants and onto the floor.

Finally, the visitor could not restrain himself. "Don't you see that it is full?" he said. "You can't get any more in!"

"Just so," replied Nan-in, stopping at last. "And like this cup, you are filled with your own ideas. How can you expect me to give you Zen unless you offer me an empty cup?"[4]

There are many important lessons in this parable. At the onset, Zen is not taught; it is an experience—a way of being. The word "Zen" is the Japanese pronunciation of the Chinese "Ch'an," which means "meditation." Fischer (2017) explains: "Not relying on scripture, doctrine or ritual, Zen is verified by personal experience and is passed on from master to disciple, hand to hand, ineffably, through hard, intimate training."[5] This philosophy of experiential learning underscores that we do not have all of the answers; each of us has a lifetime of lessons to learn. The scholar desires to prove that he is all-knowing and therefore misses the vital lesson within not-knowing. In Zen, it is the *not-knowing* that is essential for growth, becoming the empty cup *is* success.

It does not take many
words to tell the truth.
~ Thatȟáŋka Íyotake[6] ~

So how, then, do we foster an open space within ourselves to listen and learn?

Zen denotes a form of learning that is intimately personal. This paradigm and pedagogy are distinct from many Western education systems in which there is an emphasis on knowledge (as a thing) and knowing (as an experience). In other words, as previously mentioned, schools systems *test what students know* but often disregard the process of supporting *how they grow*. Essentially, they focus on information rather than on transformation. This is significant because it relates to the sacred nature of learning.

As human beings, we have the incredible ability to change and be changed. Learning—in its most liberating state—allows us to let go of preconceived notions, shifts our consciousness, stretches our ideas, and cultivates inner-standing (not under-standing). This relates, quite beautifully, to the world of Zen, and to the practice of just breathing.

What happens when we embody learning, embody breathing, embody life itself? When do you feel the presence of the breath moving through you, emptying you, enlivening you? When do you breathe with the breath? When do you honor the breath in deep appreciation for its presence in your life? The necessity of the breath is beautifully depicted in yet another Zen lesson.

> A meditation master stood by the bank of a river speaking to a group of new students. "To meditate," he said, "you need to concentrate on your breathing. When you inhale, focus completely on inhaling. When you exhale, focus completing on exhaling."
>
> "Can't we do something more interesting, some visualization or concentration exercise?" asked one student. "Breathing is so . . . boring."
>
> The master grabbed the student by the neck and thrust his head under the water. The student struggled but the master held him. After a minute, the master relented and the student emerged, gasping for air. The master smiled at his soggy charge: "Do you still think breathing is boring?"[7]

Notice that it is only when the student is gasping for air that he becomes aware of the breath and begins to appreciate it. We barely notice our breath, unless of course we, too, like the student, are struggling to breathe. Have you ever gasped for air?

Pause. Turn your focus to your breath. Give it your full attention. Notice the cool air moving through your nostrils as you inhale. Now, notice the warm air leaving your nostrils as you exhale. Pay attention to how your body receives the breath. Cherish this live-giving breath as you allow yourself to be drawn into the gentle rhythm of its movement.

Now, let's open up to some teachers of the breath. Take the time to read and re-read these pieces silently and out loud. As you read, remember to breathe with the words, allowing space for the breath within and between the verses. *What is being revealed about the breath? Reflect on your relationship to breathing in your life.*

The Breath Inside the Breath

Are you looking for me?
I am in the next seat.
My shoulder is against yours.
You will not find me in stupas, not in Indian shrine rooms,
Nor synagogues or cathedrals;
Not in masses, nor kirtans, not in legs winding
Around your own neck, nor in eating nothing but vegetables.
When you really look for me, you will see me
Instantly—
You will find me in the tiniest house of time.

Kabir says, Student, tell me, what is God?
He is the breath inside the breath.

~ *Kabir*

One Breath

From pre-eternity to post-eternity
is but a single breath,
A breath free of all these melodies
high and low.

Treasure this breath,
this moment you now enjoy,
Spending it in happiness: there is
no time for sorrow.

Once this moment has passed,
it is gone forever.
Your time is less
than the very least you can imagine.

If you spend this moment laughing,
the world will be all laughter.
But if you fall into depression,
the world will be all sorrow.

Don't give your heart to this unstable,
transitory world
With all its ups and downs,
its twists and turns.

Lighten another's heart;
be light of heart yourself,
For the highest gain in the world
is this.

Take care, Nurbakhsh,
not to hurt any heart,
For this is more valuable
than any crown or throne.
~ *Javad Nurbakhsh*

The Christ's Breath

I am a hole in a flute
that the Christ's breath moves through
listen to this music.
~ *Hafiz*

Only Breath

Not Christian or Jew or Muslim, not Hindu,
Buddhist, sufi, or zen. Not any religion

or cultural system. I am not from the East
or the West, not out of the ocean or up

from the ground, not natural or ethereal, not
composed of elements at all. I do not exist,

am not an entity in this world or the next,
did not descend from Adam and Eve or any

origin story. My place is placeless, a trace
of the traceless. Neither body nor soul.

I belong to the beloved, have seen the two
worlds as one and that one call to and know,

first, last, outer, inner, only that
breath breathing human being."

~ *Rumi*

The Sutra on the Full Awareness of Breathing

"O bhikkhus, the full awareness of breathing, if developed and practiced continuously, will be rewarding and bring great advantages. It will lead to success in practicing the Four Establishments of Mindfulness. If the method of the Four Establishments of Mindfulness is developed and practiced continuously, it will lead to success in the practice of the Seven Factors of Awakening. The Seven Factors of Awakening, if developed and practiced continuously, will give rise to understanding and liberation of the mind.

"What is the way to develop and practice continuously the method of Full Awareness of Breathing so that the practice will be rewarding and offer great benefit?

"It is like this, bhikkhus: the practitioner goes into the forest or to the foot of a tree, or to any deserted place, sits stably in the lotus position, holding his or her body quite straight, and practices like this: 'Breathing in, I know I am breathing in. Breathing out, I know I am breathing out.'

1. 'Breathing in a long breath, I know I am breathing in a long breath. Breathing out a long breath, I know I am breathing out a long breath.

2. 'Breathing in a short breath, I know I am breathing in a short breath. Breathing out a short breath, I know I am breathing out a short breath.
3. 'Breathing in, I am aware of my whole body. Breathing out, I am aware of my whole body.' He or she practices like this.
4. 'Breathing in, I calm my whole body. Breathing out, I calm my whole body.' He or she practices like this.
5. 'Breathing in, I feel joyful. Breathing out, I feel joyful.' He or she practices like this.
6. 'Breathing in, I feel happy. Breathing out, I feel happy.' He or she practices like this.
7. 'Breathing in, I am aware of my mental formations. Breathing out, I am aware of my mental formations.' He or she practices like this.
8. 'Breathing in, I calm my mental formations. Breathing out, I calm my mental formations.' He or she practices like this.
9. 'Breathing in, I am aware of my mind. Breathing out, I am aware of my mind.' He or she practices like this.
10. 'Breathing in, I make my mind happy. Breathing out, I make my mind happy.' He or she practices like this.
11. 'Breathing in, I concentrate my mind. Breathing out, I concentrate my mind.' He or she practices like this.
12. 'Breathing in, I liberate my mind. Breathing out, I liberate my mind.' He or she practices like this.
13. 'Breathing in, I observe the impermanent nature of all dharmas. Breathing out, I observe the impermanent nature of all dharmas.' He or she practices like this.
14. 'Breathing in, I observe the disappearance of desire. Breathing out, I observe the disappearance of desire.' He or she practices like this.
15. 'Breathing in, I observe the no-birth, no-death nature of all phenomena. Breathing out, I observe the no-birth, no-death nature of all phenomena.' He or she practices like this.
16. 'Breathing in, I observe letting go. Breathing out, I observe letting go.' He or she practices like this.

The Full Awareness of Breathing, if developed and practiced continuously according to these instructions, will be rewarding and of great benefit.

~ *Buddha*[8]

The breath of life is the seed within these stories, poems, and parables. They each reveal the vital nature of the breath; as Rumi points out, we are "breath breathing human beings." Breathing is not boring; it carries inspiration on its currents. Don't be so quick to take it for granted. The breath is holy and life-giving. It is a treasure leading to our awakening and sovereignty.

Some essential lessons to consider:

- All life breathes one universal breath.
- When we focus on our breathing, we move into the natural rhythms of nature.
- The breath is life-giving; it is not a waste of time.
- To attend to the breath, it is to practice gratitude for life.
- By breathing, we begin to calm our mind, still our body, and open our heart.

Personal activity:

Examine the breath through the following three lenses: objective, subjective, and intersubjective:

- The objective—*According to these writers, how is breath described?*
- The subjective—*Locate a moment when you struggled to breathe deeply. What were the circumstances?*
- The intersubjective—*How does your breathing shape your relationship with others?*

Collective practices:

As a teaching tool, we've used these texts in different learning contexts. Students find it invigorating to focus on the breath. "It was very refreshing to be a part of a class where I was given five minutes to be one with myself and focus on my breathing," shared one of Mary's students. "This process allowed for me to remove certain thoughts from my mind and make room for new wisdom."

- Select one of the above poems or verses to read slowly together. Invite participants to share a word or verse that spoke to them and the reason why.
- Create questions from the selected literary work on the breath, for instance, "What are you filled with?" or "Do you think breathing is boring?"
- Do the breathing practices from *The Sutra on the Full Awareness of Breathing*. Write or share your experiences.

These activities are not finite but rather generative, a way to help all of us move deeper into the breath. Once we start prioritizing the breath in our lives, we're able to become aware of the thoughts and emotions that either inhibit or enhance our breathing.

*As we breathe, let us enter into the vastness of the mind.
How can training our mind become part of our transformative practice?*

Notes

1. D. Levy. (2016). *Mindful Tech*. New Haven: Yale University Press, pp. 38–39.
2. A. P. Gumbs. (2020). *Undrowned: Black Feminist Lessons from Marine Mammals*. Emergent Strategy Series. Chico, CA: AK Press, p. 19.
3. A Cherokee Legend. www.firstpeople.us/.
4. E. Davy Pearmain, ed. (2007). *Doorways to the Soul: 52 Wisdom Tales from Around the World*. Eugene, OR: Resource Publications, p. 38.
5. www.lionsroar.com/what-is-zen-buddhism-and-how-do-you-practice-it/.
6. Otherwise known as Sitting Bull.
7. F. Kofman. (2006). *Conscious Business: How to Build Values Through Values*. Boulder, CO: Sounds True, p. 247.
8. T. N. Hanh. (2012). *Awakening of the Heart: Essential Buddhist Sutras and Commentaries*. Berkeley, CA: Parallax Press, pp. 10–12.

4
MENTAL EMANCIPATION

Rituals of awakening might sound like a series of activities. One more thing to do. But really, it's about stilling ourselves so we can hear the silence. Slowing ourselves down to intentionally breathe. And even finding rest for our minds.

Rest of mind is as necessary as rest of body
And yet we always keep the former in action.
~ Hazrat Inayat Khan ~

The focus of this chapter is to give ourselves space to discern and reflect on how to move towards greater wholeness. Contemplative practices can develop our mental muscles.

All that we are is the result of what we have thought;
We are formed and molded by our thoughts.
~ The Dhammapada ~

Thoughts turn into words. Words matter. Words have power. Words generate worlds. "In the beginning was the Word, and the Word was with God, and the Word was God" (Genesis 1:1). Words reflect who we are and what we think. Words are creation.

In our quietest moments, the words we tell ourselves can shape our interpretations, expressions, and manifestations. This is significant. When blindly wedded to our personal thoughts, we lose the ability to observe and direct them. In this state, we exist beholden to our ego's every desire, or as Bob Marley chants in *Pimper's Paradise*, "Every need got an ego to feed." In this milieu, we can become entrapped inside fears and worries, lust and envy. Some sages have called this the small mind.

Caught in a small mind state, we may think or feel like we are being pulled into a quagmire, where feelings and thoughts are often conditioned and aren't always the best guides to authentic relationship to reality. This mentality left unchecked causes exhaustion and drains our energy. The incessant internal chatter often distracts and depletes us from reaching higher states of consciousness and manifesting the world we want. We must remember that we have a choice.

So how then do we choose to refocus our intentions and energies?

As human beings, we have willpower. When we begin to shift our attention and focus on identifying our thoughts clearly, they begin to lose power and mental hold over us. In other words, when we are asserting authority over our lives, we establish right relationship to our thoughts, recognizing that our thoughts are merely objects in our awareness. If we are subjects of our thoughts, then we have the power. With this recognition, our thoughts have no real control over us. We each have the incredible ability to dethrone the ego so that the ego no longer reigns supreme. To emancipate in this context, then, means to set ourselves free. Freeing our minds is the precipice of sovereignty.

To build on these concepts, throughout this chapter, we will consider four essential lessons: the first is an understanding of *the mind itself*, the second is the *power of internal witness*, the third is *consciousness as agency*, and the fourth is *training the mind*. Because each of us contends with our own chattering mind, tools have been developed across time and continents that will help us train our mental faculties. And through this disciplined process of being, we gain independence; we become the authors of our own lives and agents of change.

Nothing is permanent.
Everything is subject to change.
Being is always becoming.
~ Buddha ~

What is the Mind?

For the purposes of mental emancipation, we wish to make a few distinctions between the brain, the mind, and consciousness. Although each are complex fields unto themselves, we want to offer a very brief description to clarify what we mean when we use these terms.

The Brain

The brain is a physical organ located within the human skull. Using microscopes and other technical instrumentation, it can be examined and measured. It is commonly accepted that there are actually four brains in one, each with a specific function: the hind or reptilian brain (survival), cognitive brain (emotional intelligence), neocortex (creative and complex thinking), and prefrontal lobe (reason, problem solving, and harmonization).[1] These four brains in one have evolved over time, leading to higher and more complex abilities.

The brain is also made up of left and right hemispheres joined together by a bundle of nerve fibers called the corpus callosum. The left brain is considered more verbal, analytical, and orderly than the right brain. It is better at things like reading, critical thinking, and computations. The right brain is more visual and intuitive and considered more creative, imaginative, and holistic. Moreover, it's important to recognize that the brain is alive. The brain has what's called neuroplasticity, meaning it can adapt, grow, and decline (Small, 2008). Referencing Merzenich, Doige (2007) states, "The brain is not an inanimate vessel that we fill; rather it is more like a living creature with an appetite, one that can grow and change itself with proper nourishment and exercise" (p. 47).

In *My Grandmother's Hands: Racialized Trauma and the Pathway to Mending Our Hearts and Bodies*, Resmaa Menakem (2017) presents healing that is grounded in embodied practices. "The body is where we live," (p. 7) he writes. He goes on to examine the reptilian "lizard" brain that focuses on survival and connects this with the traumas of white-body supremacy that dominate American history, institutions, and culture. *My Grandmother's Hands* is a call to action for us to recognize that racism and healing are not just in our minds but are also embedded deep within our bodies.

In addition to having four brains in one, it has been discovered that the brain contains compartments that can either debilitate or liberate. As an evolutionary process, biologist Bruce Lipton discovered, "From the simplest cells on up, a new life unfolds in one of two ways: It can either defend itself against a hostile environment or open, expand and embrace its world. It can't do both at the same time," which underscores the need for creating healthy learning environments.[2]

Given this nuanced understanding of the function of the brain and its role in healing, we need to create classroom environments where all four aspects of the brain can develop and thrive. Yet to develop these healthier learning spaces, we need to shift from a culture of fear to one of curiosity, from classrooms of control to compassion, from teaching as technocratic to transformational. To blossom in this direction, we need to tap into and become aware of the interconnected dimensions of our brain and create teaching methods, practices, and instructional spaces that encourage and support the full potential for growth.

The Mind

Although one, the mind constitutes five aspects: the unconscious (what we are unaware of), subconscious (a storehouse of buried memories, conditionings, complexes, and drives), the preconscious (what is coming into consciousness, "on the tip of my tongue"), the conscious (what is in the field of our awareness), and the supraconscious (intuitions, inner knowing, sublime inspiration). The mind stores the contents of our thoughts, feelings, emotions, and sensations and as such is connected to the ego (our point of view and experiences). However, keep in mind that the vastness of our mental faculties also unites us to our greater potential: "communication with other minds and [the] Mind-at-large" (Helminski, 2017, p. 17). It's worth considering that so much of education today is about the conscious mind—which is important—but what are we still missing? We are not unlocking our full mental powers. The mind is a wellspring of potentiality and exploration both within and between the individual and interpersonal planes. Tapping into the larger Mind develops a contemplative and more comprehensive learning praxis.

As we develop a holistic picture of the Mind, there are roadblocks. Such as the ego! What do I do with my ego? According to the yogic texts, the ego is *ahamkara* (*aham*, "self" and *kara*, "created thing," meaning the ego is the "I maker"); it is what gives us a sense of a separate self. Now, the ego is not inherently bad. It locates us in time and space and can act as a sort of alarm clock, waking us up to an unsettling feeling of anger or disgust. The ego can serve as an important catalyst for a reaction and response. The poet Sunni Patterson (2021) recently shared, "Ego is the car, but Spirit needs to be the driver." Building on this idea, Jarrett (2021) explains,

> The mind is conditioned by ego in a way that constrains conscious awareness strictly to the personal sphere of experience. In this way thoughts, feelings, emotions, and sensations as they constitute the content in consciousness become personalized as "my thoughts, feelings, emotions, and sensations" (p. 73).[3]

The "my mentality" is egotistical. So, beware that when the ego is in control, it's a danger zone for yourself and others.

Unlike the brain, the mind cannot be examined and measured under a microscope. We must look within to examine the intricate and intimate compartments of the mind and learn to traverse them, much like a labyrinth.

What are the contents (thoughts, feelings, emotions, sensations) in your mind at this very moment? Write down three words that come to mind:

1. _____.
2. _____.
3. _____.

The mind holds the words, but to interpret these three words takes consciousness.

Consciousness

Consciousness is the larger field of awareness in which the mind dwells. According to the Indian sage Ramana Maharashi, "a genuine seeker" is able to "grow beyond the mind and experience in himself the reality of Self."[4] This is the faculty of consciousness. Consciousness provides us with the ability to attend, witness, and enter into what Helminski referred to as the Mind-at-large. It is only through consciousness that we can see the contents held within our minds and instead of operating on autopilot—through habit, fear, or desire—we can consciously discern and choose a course of action. Again, according to Jarrett (2021), "A significant part of waking up involves making the mind an object in awareness and shifting our exclusive identity with it to a deeper and higher self that transcends yet includes it."[5]

To examine the mind, we may use the power of consciousness to focus and attend to its contents. Consider the three words you wrote earlier. Ask yourself: Do they belong to me? Are they useful? Are they positive or demeaning? What value do they have? I am now more fully aware of (fill in the blank):

_____
_____
_____.

Shifting our attention away from our mind into a critical consciousness can free us from being trapped within our mental state.

I'm tired of the traps within,
sometimes your brain's your cell,
prison's the skin you in.
~ Public Enemy ~

To break free from "our brain cell," we need sparks of illumination. These sparks are consciousness. Since our consciousness is grander than the mind, it gives us the ability to see the bigger picture. Our power is in our consciousness. This is why the sitting in silence, the breath work, and watching our thoughts can serve as such a life-changing practice. We're literally able to plug into a higher way of thinking. We can re-wire ourselves, but it takes a different kind of work. The work of consciousness is the power of internal witness which leads to awakening.

The Power of Internal Witness

Now that we have a basic understanding of the distinction between the brain, the mind, and consciousness, let's travel into our thoughts and begin this section with a metaphorical question: What if our internal narratives are like clouds in the sky?

Consider for a moment how quickly we get caught inside the charged thought-clouds of our mind along with the emotional and egotistical rain forming within them. Before we know it, a storm ensues and propels us from one notion to the next; in rapid succession, we are carried along thought to thought, feeling to feeling, emotion to emotion. This is akin to a storm brewing in a summer sky. These electrified onslaughts can consume us, causing fatigue, devastation, trickeries, and misdirection.

There is another way to be!

Through self-examination, we can discover that our thoughts are not fixed. Although they seem solid, they are merely fleeting illusions—ephemeral contents within a larger consciousness. As we see and study our own thoughts, the more transitory they become, akin to clouds merely passing through the vast sky on a windy day. Turning thoughts into clouds is like turning solids into liquid. The alchemy of self-discovery is within us.

> *Wherever the mind wanders,*
> *restless and diffuse in its search for satisfaction without,*
> *lead it within; train it to rest in the Self.*
> ~ The Bhagavad Gita 6:26 ~

Ponder this beautiful story found within the early Christian Desert community called *Catch the Wind*. It contains a dialogue between an elder monk and his student, for which the student is seeking counsel on how to deal with his distracting thoughts.

> A brother came to abbot pastor and said, "Many distracting thoughts come into my mind, and I am in danger because of them."
>
> Then the elder thrust him out into the open air and said, "Open up the garments about your chest and catch the wind in them."
>
> But he replied, "This I cannot do."
>
> So, the elder said to him, "If you cannot catch the wind, neither can you prevent distracting thoughts from coming into your head. Your job is to say 'No' to them."[6]

The elder shares an empowering lesson. By shifting the student's attention to what he *can* do, the wise pastor turns a perilous situation into a productive one. Stop for a moment and ask yourself, can you remember a time when you did not have thoughts moving through your mind? Even while sleeping, ideas continue to pass through as dreams. This is what thoughts do: they arise and form like clouds in our inner sky. We cannot stop this process; we cannot catch the wind of thoughts any more than we can stop the clouds from forming. Therefore, trying to do so is focusing our attention in the wrong place.

If we cannot stop the thoughts from arising, what can we do? We can ignore them, say "No" to them, or even say "Yes" to them. But we can investigate deeper and discern the motivation behind this thinking. By placing our attention and holding it on our chosen intention, we begin to strengthen our inner compass of concentration. Little by little, distracting thoughts no longer pull away our attention. As a result, we gain clearer direction and sovereignty. Listen and attune ourselves, once again, to a reggae lyric. Bob Marley chants, "Emancipate yourselves from mental slavery, none but ourselves can free our minds." As we walk to this rhythm, we slowly and steadily climb the mountain toward our own freedom.

The mind often gets mired to the past and preoccupied with the future. Yet our power exists in the present. Our locus of control: *the here and now*. The only reality *is* the present reality. For awareness to arise, it's critical that we shift our attention away from the rambling thoughts that weigh us down. Focus instead on surrendering to the vast open sky within that leads into the larger Mind of Consciousness.

> *What we pay attention to grows.*
> ~ adrienne maree brown ~

To grow gardens of empowerment, we must become masters of our mind. The thoughts and ideas we choose to sow and water shape the gardens that we grow.

Consciousness as Agency

> *The soil of our mind contains many seeds, positive and negative.*
> *We are the gardeners who identify, water, and cultivate the best seeds.*
> ~ Thich Nhat Hanh ~

A seed contains the bounties of life and yet has no energy on its own. The seed cannot create itself unless it is part of a larger ecosystem; thus, there is some level of cultivation in creation. Similarly, we have ideas and questions within that may lay dormant or become awakened in our lives. Consider that we might even be watering thoughts we actually don't want to grow. This section on *consciousness as agency* explores this concept.

Let's turn to the word *intention*.

Intention describes what we plan to do; it is an offering, a determination, a purpose, and a process of healing (Webster Dictionary, 2020). Without intention, we have no direction. So, these definitions help set the course for an inward journey wherein each of us identifies a particular focus—or seed. The healthiest seeds inside ourselves are not wedded to the ego. They have a higher—or deeper—purpose rooted to our soul. Consider asking yourself a sacred question such as *What is my purpose in life?* This question becomes the shovel that helps you dig for answers.

In the garden of self-discovery, discernment is an essential ingredient. We have to be able to identify the weeds and be willing to uproot them. These weeds can be repurposed and even fertilize new areas for growth. This is not necessarily an easy task. Some weeds look beautiful. Some of them have been a part of us our whole lives. When we uproot them, a small part of us dies for something more authentic to emerge. We might realize, for instance, that the promotion we've been fighting for is a weed, and it's time to let it go. Every reason has a season—just like in nature—and the same is true for us.

> *O mind! Be patient. Everything comes with patience.*
> *Although the gardener waters the plants hundreds of times,*
> *they bloom only when their season comes.*
> ~ Kabir ~

Planting, pausing, and patience help reveal ourselves to ourselves in a new light. The invocation to *The Chandogya Upanishad* begins with "Lead me from the unreal to the real." Similarly, one of the ten Ethiopian virtues of initiatory mastery is the ability to tell the difference between what is real and unreal. As we water what is real, we begin to bear the fruit of authenticity. Our divine purpose is to blossom into the fullness of our unique selves. And remember, all good gardens take time to grow. This is a true reflection of what occurs deep inside our bodies, hearts, and souls.

Train the Mind

Over a century ago, William James (1890) explained in *Principles of Psychology* that to have self-mastery, it's imperative to have control over your mind: "The faculty of voluntarily bringing back a wandering attention over and over again" is an "education par excellence." Critical thinking demands a focused and attentive mind. Is this level of training occurring in our schools?

The average attention span of a human being dropped from 12 seconds in 2000 to 8 seconds in 2013.[7] This is one second less than the attention span of a goldfish. And this was a study from 2013; imagine what it is today!

Many students *and* teachers together encounter the daily stressors and toxins of a miseducation system and a society that's getting busier and busier. Our attention spans are depleting, while anxiety is steadily increasing. Most school systems are built on *Chronos*—linear, measured, counted—time. time. time. tick-tock as we're chained to the clock. *Kairos*, on the other hand, measures moments (not seconds).

Our understanding of time is conditioned at a young age. The indoctrination into time itself originates inside school systems. Bells ring. Children move. The colonial clock governs instruction. By the time we graduate, many of us have internalized this worldview and have a factory mentality. This is so sad. Because learning, like our brains, is alive; it is not time-bound, linear, or static. The present moment is timeless. Our existence exists *now*. Attention (not attendance) is connected to intention. And intention is connected to interests. This is why learning is so relational. Teaching holistically is circular and dimensional, think of a spiral, and prioritizes self-discovery, which requires we reevaluate our relationship to time.

38 Mental Emancipation

In fact, in both the East and West, the sole purpose of education was the transformation of the whole student (body-mind-heart-soul); it was a way for students to search for the ultimate meaning and purpose in their lives. It was through stillness, beholding, and contemplation that students had the time, space, and energy to fully engage in their learning, not for the sake of a grade but for the sake of wisdom itself.

In reality, many of us are constrained by institutions. How, then, do we facilitate meaning-making within structured bureaucracies and mandated time blocks? What purpose is guiding our praxis?

The Buddha teaches that to train the mind (quick, fickle, and difficult to focus) is to act with consciousness. This is the only way to free the mind's race-old urges and proddings. But this kind of training, Mahatma Gandhi warned, "requires the patience of someone trying to empty the sea with a teacup."[8] Nevertheless, because our brains our malleable, we can practice concentration and actually increase our levels of focus. But how? Sincere listening. And even devoting time to reading has been measured as an effective tool. Each of these is applicable to classroom practice.

So is meditation: even in stringent conditions—like having 50 minutes in a high school classroom with 30+ students—we can intentionally pivot inward and unearth our capabilities. Mindfulness is precious; it is the fertile ground of growing consciousness. If it's three minutes or 300 hours, that's not what matters. The key is being fully present to the present. In this mental state, we open to *Kairos* time. Here, then, in this moment, we are able to disarm the tick-tock of the clock.

To examine the mind, a person needs
to use the power of consciousness to focus
and attend to the contents within one's mind.
~ Jean Gebser[9] ~

Learning propels us inward *and* outward. In school, we are trained to find answers outside ourselves. Books. Periodicals. Exams. Anything and everything within our external reach. Yes, even our eyes look to the world, and our hands stretch outward. But what if education is really an internal quest, deeply connected and embedded to mental emancipation? As teachers, how do we encourage critical consciousness and operationalize rituals of awakening?

Consider the misnomer that a math teacher teaches math. If a teacher starts with math (the content), they often engage only the students who are already inclined toward mathematics. But when the teacher begins with the students (as subjects), then the path to math becomes more humane and accessible. This significant shift moves students into the center of learning. Now, math becomes a tool for the students rather than the students being mere containers for the math.

Unfortunately, teachers are often trained in content expertise (the science of our profession) yet are rarely equipped with subjective and intersubjective techniques of belonging. Classrooms that nurture collective consciousness embody experiential modes of connection, communication, community building, compassion, and commitment (Watson, 2012).

As we go into the "living classroom," pedagogy becomes a vehicle that transports students from the personal mind to the "Mind-at-large," as Helminski reminds us. The mind-mesh of *me* to the grandeur witness of the *I*. As students experience this larger consciousness, they, too, get changed by the journey. Like Ms. Frizzle in *The Magic School Bus*, in the example given next, Mary took her students into stories to experience them firsthand (Keator, 2020). This voyage was intentional, powerful, and adventurous. She writes,

> I wanted my students to bend their ears towards the heart of the text, towards their own heart and the hearts of one another and listen without deviation. I wanted them to develop the courage to enter more deeply into what they were hearing, to face it and embrace it, rather than to shy away from it. I wanted my students to learn how to develop and strengthen their ability to listen and discern the inner voices of the stories we read in class as well as their own subjective experiences in response to these stories (p. 81).

This example accentuates the need to take students inside. Inside the book. Inside themselves. Inside their own knowing and being. The internal process awakens students to their own unique authentic voice. Each voice then becomes a fine-tuned instrument in the larger choir of awakening.

Harmonious classrooms are interpersonal and dialogic. Through this communal learning process, something new and different is created. It's like a whole new sound of togetherness. As another example of this pedagogy, Vajra describes a critical literary arts program, Sacramento Area Youth Speaks (SAYS),[10] that brings poet-mentor educators into schools (Watson, 2016). She shares,

> Today, all desks are assembled in a circle and the SAYS guidelines are on the board. Students sluggishly enter class after lunch. They are met by MmaMma Laura, a poet-mentor educator, who smiles wide as she shakes hands, gives fist bumps, and even offers a few hugs to each sixth grader. Without direction, the students go to the SAYS box and collect their journals. A few anxiously check inside their notebooks to see if there is a personalized note of response from MmaMma Laura. With their notebooks and pencils in place, the students take a seat. MmaMma Laura kindly reminds me, as well as the classroom teacher, to join the group.

> After a momentary check-in, MmaMma Laura, as the students call her, begins the writing workshop in a soothing monotone. She speaks rather slowly: "Write what I am about to tell you in your journal and then keep on writing." She provides the writing prompt: "When I look in the mirror. . . ."
>
> After just five-minutes of "free-writing" in journals in absolute silence MmaMma Laura asks "her babies" to share. Hands raise. Within minutes, the classroom is filled with young people's raw testimonies about who they are becoming in the world. There are no put-downs or laughs. Rather, a sacred solemnness fills the air and the only thing to do is stay present and hold space for one another as each voice takes center stage. These acts of vulnerability are cathartic for the speaker and also create camaraderie amongst the class (pp. 311–312).

Both Mary and Vajra's work underscore ways to develop classroom spaces that humanize. They are among an array of scholars from many disciplines coming to similar conclusions. Bache (2008) explains, "Class discussions can be structured to more effectively mobilize the collective knowledge in the room harvesting and cross-fertilizing student input to bring forward new levels of collective insight" (p. 385).

We need more of this.

Unfortunately, very few teacher training programs are wedded to critical love, radical justice, and cooperative inquiry. This impacts the entire profession and the very meaning of schooling. The word education (not schooling) derives from Latin *educare*, which reinforces the importance of drawing something out of students—versus the banking way of depositing information. Freire (1970) expounds upon this idea in *Pedagogy of the Oppressed*: "Dialogue further requires an intense faith in humankind, faith in their power to make and remake, to create and re-create, faith in their vocation to be more fully human (which is not the privilege of an elite, but the birthright of all)" (p. 71).

While education has roots to liberation, schooling does not. And when classrooms succumb to the manufactured model of learning, we miss the essence and purpose of knowledge. When the content is irrelevant, transactional, and technocratic, students often lose their humanity as they are conditioned to adapt into an assembly line of lesson plans. The industrialization of schooling robs us and our students of sacred purpose.

Given today's classroom dynamics, how do we train the mind? We can prioritize and further value intention, attention, concentration, and imagination. It's been said that *there's nothing new under the sun*. Contemplative pedagogy and practices were central in the monastic traditions around the world. This is because they were aware of the detrimental and deleterious nature of an untrained mind. As Buddha advises, "More than those who hate you, more than all your enemies, an undisciplined mind does greater harm" (3: 42). The mind can be a force of mental entrapment. Thus, each of us has an inner prison as well as the key to our own sovereignty.

If you control the diameter of a person's mind,
you will control the circumference of their behavior.
~ Elijah Muhammad ~

The amazing reality: freedom is within reach. Liberation is educational. This kind of pedagogy requires multidimensional thinking grounded in the physical, historical, material, cultural, political, psychological, mental and emotional worlds. At this intersection exists a transcendent spiritual unification of disciplines—connecting through the ultimate manifestation of abolition.[11]

From *Public Enemy* to *The Bhagavad Gita*, there exist lessons that allow us to break free from the shackles of mental captivity. Essentially, each of us has inner storms, but we're also equipped with an inner compass to navigate them. Stories can serve as a map that leads us back to ourselves. These teachings reconnect us with an ancient, eternal path of self-discovery.

Our legacy is louder than the ivory tower
Older than borders that divided us into being something we are not

Somehow we forgot
To put tongue in rightful place
Use words to transform space

When minds are unlocked
Tongues get free
Free to speak truth fully

So hear we be
From privilege and poverty
Accepting no praise or pity
Just mouth-full of poetry
Centered in space
Speaking between the past and this place

Future
Calling us forward
For inside us
Lives the next generation

Now choose
Genocide or Education
~ Vajra M. Watson ~

42 Mental Emancipation

Reimagine education inside our classrooms, communities, nations, and even—*within ourselves*. Reestablish healthy boundaries that create, regenerate, and balance. Make choices that nourish us and our students. Ma Jaya Sati Bhagavati teaches, "Learn to drink as you pour, so the spiritual heart cannot run dry and you always have love to give."

As you journey into the parables presented next, be cognizant of your inner thoughts, ideas, attachments, and embedded assumptions. *What is being revealed about your beliefs? Do your beliefs serve as borders that inhibit connection? Reflect on the workings of the mind in your life. Are you in control of your mind or is your mind in control of you?*

~~~~~

The Two Wolves

One evening an old Cherokee told his grandson about a battle that goes on inside people. He said, "My son, the battle is between two wolves inside us all.

"One is Evil—It is anger, envy, jealousy, sorrow, regret, greed, arrogance, self-pity, guilt, resentment, inferiority, lies, false pride, superiority, and ego.

"The other is Good—It is joy, peace, love, hope, serenity, humility, kindness, benevolence, empathy, generosity, truth, compassion and faith."

The grandson thought about it for a minute and then asked his grandfather, "Which wolf wins?"

The old Cherokee simply replied, "The one you feed."

~ *Cherokee Tale*[12]

Do Not Open the Door

A student once asked his rabbi for help. "I try to study and pray," he said, "but distracting, troubling thoughts are always coming into my head, and I cannot control them."

"What would you do," asked the rabbi, "if you saw from your window that a person was coming to your home whom you did not wish to talk with. Would you let him in?"

"I would not open the door. I would tell them to go away," the student replied.

"Exactly," said the rabbi. "You must be aware of your thoughts when they are at your mind's door and simply turn them away."

~ *Hasidic Tale*[13]

The Mind

As an archer aims an arrow, the wise aim their restless thoughts, hard to aim, hard to restrain.

As a fish hooked and left on the sand thrashes
About in agony, the mind being trained in meditation
trembles all over, desperate to escape the hand of Mara.[14]

Hard it is to train the mind, which goes where it
Likes and does what it wants. But a trained mind
Brings health and happiness. The wise can direct
their thoughts, subtle and elusive, wherever they
choose: a trained mind brings health and happiness.

Those who can direct their thoughts, which are
Unsubstantial and wander so aimlessly, are freed
From the bonds of Mara.

They are not wise whose thoughts are not steady

And minds not serene, who do not know dharma,
The law of life. They are wise whose thoughts
Are steady and minds serene, unaffected by good
And bad. They are awake and free from fear.

Remember, this body is like a fragile clay pot.
Make your mind a fortress and conquer Mara with
The weapon of wisdom. Guard your conquest always.
Remember that this body will soon lie in the earth

Without life, without value, useless as a burned log.

~ *Buddha*[15]

Watching Thought

The thought manifests as the word,
The word manifests as the deed,
The deed develops into habit,
And the habit hardens into character,
So watch the thought
And its ways with care,
And let it spring from love
Born out of respect for all beings.

~ *John P. Miller*[16]

In these texts, an underlying message emerges. Everyone struggles with the nafs of the mind. In the Sufi tradition, the nafs are anger, envy, arrogance, and ego just like in the Cherokee story.

Our job is to first identify them through the practice of observing them and then conquer them through disciplinary focus and self-study. The rabbinic story *Do not open the door* is a powerful reminder that each of us has the power to say *No* to the distracting thoughts that consume our attention, time, and energy. That is, once we realize them. In *The Dhammapada* chapter titled "The Mind," the Buddha likens the training of the mind to an archer and calls forth the guiding "weapon of wisdom." The habits of the mind shape all aspects of our behavior. Mastery of the mind is a precursor to enlightenment.

> *One does not become enlightened by imagining figures of light*
> *But by making the darkness conscious.*
> ~ Carl Gustav Jung ~

To go toward the light is an important metaphor. Consider that when you stand with your back to the sun, your shadow is before you; but when you turn and face the sun, your shadow falls behind you. This describes the difference between the dormant and illuminated soul. In other words, this is primarily a difference of will, not capability. When someone is under the sway of external influences, they can easily be deceived by the mind and therefore forget their soul.

Visualize a woman leaning over a bridge, gazing into the depths of the ocean. She can only see reflections and shadows. She thinks this is the reality of the sea because it is all she is able to see. Subsequently, she becomes caught inside the web of illusion, nothing but the shadow of real vibrations. When this same woman turns spiritually inward, the shadow-thoughts and the shadow-words and the shadow-interests fade into nescience. The mind-mesh of divisions fades. The entire attention becomes an experience in Unity. Unity of self with purpose. Unity of self with the world. This is the meaning of the Sufi invocation: "Toward the One, the Perfection of Love, Harmony and Beauty, the Only Being; United with All the Illuminated Souls, Who form the Embodiment of the Master, the Spirit of Guidance."[17]

May we remember our sacred power by focusing our attention inward onto our heart's deepest desire. In this newfound sovereignty, we begin creating space to consider the perspectives of others. As we do, we radically embrace bolder horizons.

Some essential lessons to consider:

- There are important distinctions between the brain, mind, and consciousness.
- Witnessing one's thoughts develops awareness of them.

Mental Emancipation

- It takes commitment, discipline, and effort to train the mind.
- Traditions all over the world recognize the importance of training the mind toward critical consciousness.
- There are pedagogies and practices that can develop student's mental capacities and capabilities.

Personal activity:

Sit still and quiet for a few moments and watch the thoughts pass through your mind as if they are clouds passing through the sky. Now, in the below circle, write all the thoughts inside your mind.

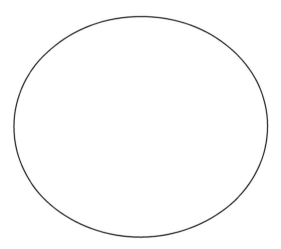

1. What do you notice about your thoughts?
2. How are you being shaped by them?
3. What is inside your mind?
4. What messages do you receive from your family or society?

What thoughts nourish you?
What thoughts deplete you?
See them.
Choose them.
Only water
What you want to grow.
~ Mary and Vajra~

Collective practices:

The modern Indian sage Ramana Maharashi once defined a genuine seeker as someone who has "a constant and passionate longing to break free from life's sorrow—not by running away from it, but by growing beyond his mind and experiencing in himself the reality of Self."[18] The training of the mind is not about more information; it is about inner transformation. Therefore, it's critical that we are active participants. There are a number of ways to utilize these lessons on the mind in your daily life or as a teaching tool in multiple learning contexts. Here are three questions to contemplate individually and as a group.

- The objective—*According to the stories above, how is the mind described?*
- The subjective—*How do you train your mind? What do you find challenging in training your mind?*
- The intersubjective—*How is a trained mind valued or not valued in your culture or religious or spiritual tradition? How can training the mind benefit the whole?*

Here is another lesson to utilize in the classroom. Before or after reading the selected stories about the wolf, the rabbi, and the archer, ask students to write down the lyrics to a song that inspires them or a song that they currently have "on repeat." This activity is about what plays in our heads (internally and externally) and what we're watering inside the gardens of our minds.

- What are the words of the lyrics? What is being said and conveyed?
- How does what we hear impact who we are becoming?
- Share your music and share your lyrics with the group. What is the collective, lyrical compilation of our lives?

These activities provide a scaffolded approach to mindfulness. They are just examples. The ultimate goal is to unlock ourselves from thinking our way is the *only* way. Freedom and liberation are both individual and collective. As we become aware of our inner power to witness our thoughts, we expand and develop the capacity to welcome into our lives the perspective of others. This opening gives birth to new realities.

Where does the body end and the mind begin?
Where does the mind end and the spirit begin?
They cannot be divided as they are interrelated
and are but different aspects
of the same all-pervading divine consciousness.
~ B.K.S. Iyengar ~

Let's go there now. Turn the page.

Notes

1. See more information in Sharon Begley, Joseph Chilton Pearce, The HeartMath Institute.
2. This quote is in J. C. Pearce. (2004). *The Biology of Transcendence*. Rochester, VT: Park Street Press, p. 116.
3. L. Jarrett. (2021). *Deepening Perspectives on Chinese Medicine*. Stockbridge, MA: Spirit Path Press, p. 73.
4. This quote comes from S. Mitchell. (1993). *The Enlightened Mind*. New York: HarperPerennial, p. xiii.
5. L. Jarrett. (2021). *Deepening Perspectives on Chinese Medicine*. Stockbridge, MA: Spirit Path Press, p. 73.
6. E. Davy Pearmain, ed. (2007). *Doorways to the Soul: 52 Wisdom Tales from Around the World*. Eugene, OR: Resource Publications, p. 25.
7. According to the National Center for Biotechnology Information at the U.S. National Library of Medicine.
8. E. Easwaran. (2007). *The Dhammapada*. Tomales, CA: Nilgiri Press, p. 111.
9. J. Gebser. (1985). *The Ever-Present Origin*. Athens, OH: Ohio University Press, kindle edition. See Gebser's thoughts on the nature of time-freedom or achronicity.
10. For more information visit, SAYS at says.ucdavis.edu.
11. See F. Fanon. (1963). *The Wretched of the Earth*, trans. C. Farrington. London: Grove Press; B. Love. (2019). *We Want to Do More Than Survive: Abolitionist Teaching the Pursuit of Educational Freedom*. Boston, MA: Beacon Press.
12. A Cherokee Legend. www.firstpeople.us.
13. E. Davy Pearmain, ed. (2007). *Doorways to the Soul: 52 Wisdom Tales from Around the World*. Eugene, OR: Resource Publications, p. 25.
14. Mara is the tempter, the embodiment of temptations and selfish attachments in the Buddhist tradition.
15. E. Easwaran, trans. (2007). *The Dhammapada*. Tomales, CA: Nilgiri Press, pp. 115–116.
16. J. P. Miller. (2000). *Education and the Soul: Towards a Spiritual Curriculum*. Albany, NY: SUNY Press, p. 6.
17. Adapted from the Sufi *Bowl of Saki*. Teachings of January 4.
18. quoted in S. Mitchell. (1993). *The Enlightened Mind*. New York: HarperPerennial, p. xiii.

5
EXPANDING PERSPECTIVES

I need other people, who have sampled other parts of the world.
Together we can make a more complete picture.
I need to report my piece of reality honestly, listen to others,
and remember that the bit of truth I know is not anywhere near all the truth there is.
~ Donella Meadows ~[1]

As we continue to turn our attention toward the mind, we begin to see the barrage of thoughts passing through it, one thought after another in a seemingly never-ending stream. Each thought—a charged cloud—passing through the open sky of mental space, carrying potential lightning bolts of emotions that trigger anxiety, anger, sadness, and stress. Upon closer examination, we begin to notice that these thoughts are not only fleeting and ephemeral but also deeply personal. Each telling and retelling *the story of me*. My woes, my pain, my worries, and my fears; my loves, my hopes, my beliefs, and my dreams.

The Dhammapada opens with, "All that we are is the result of all that we have thought; We are formed and molded by our thoughts." What this ancient Buddhist text points out is that we are, in fact, what we think. Our thoughts shape the way we see ourselves, others, and the world we inhabit. Our thoughts are shaped by personal experience, history, culture, gender, etc. Focusing on our own thoughts can be beautiful, but it can also be a trap. This is because our thoughts are shaped by our own insular worldview. We are more than our thoughts, more than the sum of our thoughts.

We don't see things as they are, we see things as we are.
~ Anaïs Nin ~

How do we expand our minds to include new perspectives and horizons? Our worldview, like a set of eyeglasses, shapes what we see. It shapes our clarity of vision, and perception. What if the glasses we look through are limiting our point of view? What if our lenses are near-sighted? Where are our blind spots? How does our partial perspective limit our transformation into a fuller humanity?

These questions guide this chapter.

As we open our mind, we can more fully consider other perspectives. In actuality, life is all about perspectives. If all we ever understand is through our own limited lenses, we will continue to repeat patterns over and over again. In *The Science of Self-Empowerment: Awakening the new human story*, Braden (2017) notes that we are faced with a crisis of thinking. He questions, "How can we make room for the new world that's emerging if we are clinging to the old world of the past?" (p. 222). His question is key and relates to the portal we discussed earlier. If we cannot release our old ways of knowing, we will likely not have the capacity to conceive of anything different and new. As Einstein famously shared, "A new type of thinking is essential if mankind is to survive and move to higher levels."

Alternative paradigms offer us places for further growth. All of us can get so wedded to our own perspective, our own private movie—*the movie of me*—playing 24 hours a day, seven days a week, 365 days a year. We have this internal script playing, but that's not all. We also live in an external movie, bombarded with messages from society. The world today is very loud. From commercials to social media posts like Facebook messages, Twitter feeds, IG, Telegram, and TikTok, the barrage is non-stop.

When we carve out spaces of silence, we can hear ourselves more clearly. Do you ever stop? Slow down? Take a moment to pause. In this moment, close your eyes and take a deep breath. Now, turn within and notice your thoughts.

How many ideas contain the word "me," "my," "mine," or "I"? When our mind space is filled with our own personal agendas, there is little room left to listen. In fact, the painful truth is that most people don't listen.

To listen to others is not just to open one's physiological ears; it is much deeper. We live in internal and external echo chambers. Most of us live within our comfort zones and listen to people we already agree with. Learning is a process of opening one's mind, one's heart, and one's whole being while being open to change.

In *Nourishing Destiny*, acupuncturist Lonny Jarrett (2015) explains the Chinese character *ting* (to listen) as follows:

> The character *ting* (listen 聽) is composed of the character that stands for the rectitude of the heart (惪) combined with that for the ear (耳) of the disciple who is listening attentively to the sage (王). The overall sense imparted by this character is that, through attentive listening, one's heart may be rectified. From the imagery of the character *ting*, we might define that ability to 'listen' as the ability to hear our hearts and the hearts of others without deviation.

Applying this principle of active attentive listening, consider the dialogue between Confucius and his student in the story, *The Fasting of the Heart*.[2] Yen Hui, the pupil of Confucius, is aware that the Prince of Wei is treating his people poorly. Yet Yen Hui yearns for justice. When he tells his teacher Confucius that he wants to confront the Prince of Wei, he is told not to do it. Confucius warns that the Prince of Wei is

> convinced that he alone is right. He may pretend outwardly to take an interest in an objective standard of justice, but do not be deceived by his expression. He is not accustomed to being opposed by anyone. His way is to reassure himself that he is right by trampling on other people. . . . He may pretend to be interested in your talk about what is objectively right, but interiorly he will not hear you, and there will be no change whatsoever. You will get nowhere with this.

The student, Yen Hui, wants answers.

Confucius insists, "You must *fast!*" and then goes on to describe the fasting of the heart. "The goal of fasting is inner unity. This means hearing, but not with the ear; hearing, but not with understanding; hearing with the spirit, with your whole being." Confucius continues with the lesson:

> The hearing that is only in the ears is one thing. The hearing of the understanding is another. But the hearing of the spirit is not limited to any one faculty, to the ear, or to the mind. Hence it demands the emptiness of all the faculties. And when the faculties are empty, then the whole being listens. . . . Fasting of the heart begets unity and freedom.

In your own life, when have you been closed off like the Prince of Wei? When is a time that you've wanted to actively confront an injustice like Yen Hui? Along this spectrum, have you ever paused and "gone inside" like Confucius directs? Have you ever fasted and looked within to see what is driving your thoughts and actions? According to these teachings, listening involves way more than the ears. It is only through active, attentive, mind-body-heart hearing that we can enter into an openness that can prepare us for intersubjective dialogue, which can guide and awaken us into a more subtle and profound *I-Thou* relationship (Buber, 1970).

There are levels of listening. One level of listening is to acknowledge or reiterate what someone said. Even though we are actively listening, there is a door inside ourselves that remains closed, securely walled off from breaking open to something new. Listening takes on new meaning when it is no longer just about hearing another perspective but a complete opening. It is often jarring and disruptive. It disrupts our comfort zone, our way of seeing ourselves and the world around us. It's a huge trust walk.

People only see what they are prepared to see.
~ Ralph Waldo Emerson ~

Another level of listening is connected to learning, maturing, and transforming. When we engage in radical vulnerability, we open ourselves to receive another person's perception of the world. Through this intimate process, we go *through* someone else's perspective, and in the process, our own horizon expands. As we widen our thinking, we become skilled at holding other points of view. A fuller picture begins to emerge.

The Blind Men and the Elephant is a story from an ancient Buddhist text called the *Udàna* that offers a cautionary reminder about the ways we limit ourselves and dismiss each other:

> A large gray elephant stood eating the lush greenery in an ancient, walled garden. It paused for a moment and trumpeted loudly. Just then, three blind men came along.
> "What made that sound?" asked the first man.
> The second replied knowingly, "That sound was made by an elephant."
> "What is an elephant?" asked the third.
> "I am not completely certain," said the first man. "We should investigate."
> The first blind man went forward with his fingers outstretched until he reached the elephant's rear. His hand moved along the elephant's tail, which graced its posterior slope. "Aha!" he said. "An elephant is thin and long, just like a dangling rope."
> The second blind man went forward with his fingers outstretched until he arrived at the elephant's head. His hand moved along the elephant's ear, which rippled with thick, heavy hide. "You are wrong!" he said. "An elephant is not at all like a rope. Just like a rug, it's wide!"
> The third blind man went forward with his fingers outstretched until he reached the elephant's knee. His hand moved along the elephant's leg. He measured the girth of its thigh. You are wrong," he said. "An elephant is not like a rope or a rug. Just like a pillar, it's high!"
>
> "An elephant is like a rope!" screamed the first.
> "An elephant is like a rug!" shouted the second.
> "An elephant is like a pillar!" insisted the third.
>
> They began to pound each other and yell.
>   "A rope! A rug! A pillar!
>   "A rope! A rug! A pillar!
>   "A rope! A rug! A pillar!
> Meanwhile,
>   The elephant stood inside the walled garden,
>   Nibbling the leaves of a tree.
>   His ivory tusks curved towards the sky,
>   A miraculous sight to see.

> With billowing minds and bellowing mouths
> > To opinions these blind men held fast.
> While the elephant stood, quite undefined,
> > In the garden of ancient past.[3]

Many lessons can be gleaned from this parable. One such lesson is that the individuals in this story are blind and therefore had to rely on their other senses to comprehend the vastness of an elephant. Although listening first brought them to the elephant, they did not rely on listening to investigate further. Instead, they relied on their tactile sensibilities and filtered it through their own egos and limited viewpoints. This led them on a path toward violent conflict.

Another lesson is that we, too, are blind to other's perspectives. Consider for a moment, what is the elephant you are currently trying to name, decipher, and understand? How do you probe into other people's versions of reality? Often, we can get caught up defending our own point of view rather than listening to another. When we cannot personally experience something or someone, listening becomes our most powerful tool to gain perspective. Listening is the lens that allows us to see more clearly. Holding too tight to our own piece, we often miss the whole.

What if truth is like an elephant? The elephant does not need to change; rather, our perspective does. And what if we need the insight of others to see the full picture? Different perspectives can lead us on a path toward conflict or lead us on a path toward compassion. Consider this next story.

The Difference Between Heaven and Hell

Long ago in Japan an old woman wanted to see for herself the difference between heaven and hell. The monks in the temple agreed to grant her request. "First you shall see hell," they said as they put a blindfold over her eyes.

When the blindfold was removed, the old woman stood at the entrance to a great hall. The hall was filled with round tables, each piled high with the most delicious feast: meats, vegetables, fruits of every kind, and desserts to make your mouth water. The old woman noticed that there were people seated just out of arm's reach of the tables. Their bodies were thin, and their pale faces convulsed with frustration. They held chopsticks almost three feet long. With their chopsticks, they could reach their food, but they could not get the food back into their mouths. As the old woman watched, a hungry, angry sound rose into the air. "Enough," she said. "Let me see heaven."

When the blindfold was removed the second time, the old woman rubbed her eyes. For there she stood again at the entrance to a great hall with tables piled high with the same sumptuous feast. Again, she saw the people sitting just out of arm's reach of the food with those long chopsticks.

But the people in heaven were plump and rosy cheeked, and as she watched, the musical sound of laughter filled the air. And then the old woman laughed, for now she understood the difference. The people in heaven were using those three-feet-long chopsticks to feed each other.[4]

An important take-away from this story is that although the setting was exactly the same—they each have food, each other, and long chopsticks—the difference is not in what they have but in how they see and use what they have. The first group is solely focused on feeding themselves. They have a "me-my" perspective that leads to starvation. The second group is aware of one another and the limitations of feeding themselves. So when they shift their perspective away from self to encompass a "we-our" worldview, they discover food, joy, nourishment and each other.

What if our reality does not need to change, but rather our perception of that reality? Answers to this question can be found across time, cultures and continents. Next we present some teachings that can broaden our horizons. These literary pieces highlight both the limitations and the power of our perceptions. Take the time to read and re-read these pieces silently and out loud, personally and collectively. As you experience these texts, remember that no one person has the full view. So how, then, do you challenge yourself to listen to the body, mind, and heart of someone else?

Learning is not about talking; learning is linked to listening.

―――

Life Through My Eyes

Life through my bloodshot eyes
Would scare a square to death
Poverty, murder, violence
And never a moment 2 rest
Fun and games R few
But treasured like gold to me
Cuz I realize that I must return
2 my spot in poverty
But mock my words when I say
My heart will not exist
Unless my destiny comes through
And puts an end 2 all of this
    ~ *Tupac Amaru Shakur*

A Man, His Son, and the Donkey

A man and his son were once going with their Donkey to market. As they were walking along by its side, a countryman passed them and said: "You fools, what is a Donkey for but to ride upon?"

So, the Man put the Boy on the Donkey, and they went on their way. But soon they passed a group of men, one of whom said: "See that lazy youngster; he lets his father walk while he rides."

So, the Man ordered his Boy to get off and got on himself. But they hadn't gone far when they passed two women, one of whom said to the other: "Shame on that lazy lout to let his poor little son trudge along."

Well, the Man didn't know what to do, but at last he took his Boy up before him on the Donkey. By this time, they had come to the town, and the passers-by began to jeer and point at them. The Man stopped and asked what they were scoffing at. The men said: "Aren't you ashamed of yourself for overloading that poor Donkey of yours—you and your hulking son?"

The Man and Boy got off and tried to think what to do. They thought and they thought, till at last they cut down a pole, tied the Donkey's feet to it, and raised the pole and the Donkey to their shoulders. They went along amid the laughter of all who met them till they came to Market Bridge, when the Donkey, getting one of his feet loose, kicked out and caused the Boy to drop his end of the pole. In the struggle, the Donkey fell over the bridge, and because his four feet were tied together, he drowned.

"That will teach you," said an old man who had followed them:
"Please all, and you will please none."
~ Aesop Fables

The Red and Blue Coat

There once were two childhood friends who were determined to remain that way forever. When they were grown, they each married and built their houses facing one another. Just a small path formed a border between their farms.

One day a trickster from the village decided to test their friendship. He dressed himself in a two-color coat that was divided down the middle: red on the right side and blue on the left side.

Wearing this coat, the man walked along the narrow path between the two houses. The two friends were each working opposite each other in the fields. The trickster made enough noise as he traveled between them to cause each friend to look up from his side of the path at the same moment and notice him.

At the end of the day, one friend said to the other, "Wasn't that a beautiful red coat that man was wearing today?"

"No," replied the other. "It was a blue coat."

"I saw that man clearly as he walked between us!" said the first, "His coat was red."
"You are wrong!" the second man said, "I saw it, too. It was blue."
"I know what I saw!" insisted the first man. "The coat was red."
"You don't know anything," replied the second man angrily. "It was blue!"
"So," shouted the first, "you think I am stupid? I know what I saw. It was red!"
"Blue!" the other man said.
"Red!" "Blue! "Red!" "Blue!"
They began to beat each other and roll around on the ground.

Just then the trickster returned and faced the two men, who were punching and kicking each other and shouting, "Our friendship is over!"

The trickster walked directly in front of them, displaying his coat. He laughed loudly at their silly fight. The two friends saw that his two-colored coat was divided down the middle, blue on the left and red on the right.

The two friends stopped fighting and screamed at the trickster, saying, "We have lived side by side all our lives like brothers! It is all *your* fault that we are fighting! You started a war between us."

"Don't blame me for the battle," replied the trickster. "I did not *make* you fight. *Both* of you are wrong, and *both* of you are right. Yes, what each one saw was true! You are fighting because you only looked at my coat from your *own* point of view."[5]

~ Congolese Tale

A Dispute in Sign Language

A Zen master and his one-eyed student lived together in a monastery. One day a wandering monk came to the Zen master and said, "If you will accept me, I wish to study with you."

The old monk replied, "Decide first if you belong here. Go into the garden and speak to my student. Converse with him in any way you wish. After that, come and tell me your decision."

The visiting monk nervously went out into the garden and saw the one-eyed monk meditating. "I will show him how profound I can be," thought the visitor. "I will converse with him in sign language."

Approaching quietly, the visiting monk tapped the one-eyed monk on the shoulder and held up one finger. The one-eyed monk held up two fingers. In response, the visiting monk held up three fingers. The one-eyed monk held up his fist. When the visiting monk saw this, he dashed out of the garden to tell the old monk his decision.

He came upon the old monk at his chores and gasped, "I do not deserve to stay here! I am unworthy of being a fellow student with the enlightened young monk I met in the garden!"

The old monk paused in his work and asked incredulously, "Are you speaking of the young one-eyed monk in the garden?"

"Yes!" exclaimed the visitor. "His knowledge is far superior to mine. I will humbly leave."

"Please tell me what happened in the garden," said the old monk, wide-eyed with amazement.

The visitor explained, "I approached the venerable monk and decided to converse in sign language. I held up one finger to indicate the Buddha. Whereupon he held up two fingers to indicate the Buddha and his teaching, the *Dharma*. I persevered in the discussion, however, and held up three fingers to show the Buddha, the *Dharma*, and the *Sangha*, the community.

Then he revealed the limitations of my understanding. He held up his fist to show me that they are all one. I immediately ran here to tell you I must leave." With a sigh, he turned and left the temple.

A moment later the young one-eyed monk stumbled into the temple. He grumbled and shouted, "Where is that scoundrel? How dare he insult me!"

"Calm your temper," said the old monk. "Please tell me what happened in the garden."

The young monk explained, "I was peacefully meditating when that rude visitor interrupted my concentration. When I looked up at him, he held up one finger, indicating that I have only one eye. I held up two fingers, politely congratulating him that he has two eyes. Then he insulted me further! He held up three fingers, pointing out that there were only three eyes among us. I could bear it no longer. I raised my fist to punch him in the nose, and he ran away!"[6]

~ Japanese Tale

The Ant in Love

Walking one day in a lonely place, King Solomon chanced upon an ant hill. All the ants immediately came out by the thousands to hail the king. Only one of their numbers took no notice of him, for it was busy carrying off grain by grain the enormous pile of sand rising before it. King Solomon called the insect before him and said:

"O tiny ant, even with the longevity of Noah and the patience of Job, you will never make this mountain of sand disappear!"

"O great King," said the ant, "do not regard my size alone . . . but take heed of my ardor as well. Behind this mound stands my beloved. Nothing shall stop me from leveling it. And if I must lose my life, at least I shall die in the hope of reaching her."

>O King, learn from an ant what the power of love is,
>learn from a blind man the secret of vision.[7]
>
>~ Persian Tale

Which story spoke to you today?

The rapper Tupac challenges us to see the world through his bloodshot eyes that have experienced the pains of poverty, violence, and murder. An environment with little rest that puts his soul to the test. Our struggles shape our outlook.

In the next story, the father and son are also challenged. They are constantly trying to appease other people while disregarding their own intuition. Their longing for the approval of others influenced them to lose their precious donkey. When we rely on external viewpoints and external validation, we often lose sight of our own desires and, consequently, make mistakes and missteps. In this Greek parable, the father and the son forsake the donkey, its value, and their dignity.

At the other extreme, if we are consumed by our perspective and do not hold space for others, we can walk blindly through life and miss so much. If we only seek the *right* answer, we run the risk of pushing people out of our lives—even our closest friends. So, in the next story, the trickster did not make the neighbors fight; he simply forced them to reconcile different points of view. Ironically, they were *both right*. Two different experiences and conclusions can exist simultaneously.

The Dispute in Sign Language reminds us that language is not always spoken; we also communicate with our bodies. Accurate interpretations are fundamental to dialogue. When we make assumptions, we lose perspective. Our interpretations reveal our inner development. Conflict is inevitable. However, when disagreements surface, we can become either like the one-eyed monk or the visitor to the temple. The key is not to miss out on an opportunity to learn.

The final parable helps us understand the importance of each person's perspective. The ant and the king have different vantage points and life experiences. Often, we take advice from those with authority. People with credentials or particular high-level positions (like the king) can seem more valuable; this is a serious problem. Some of the purest pearls of wisdom emerge from the most unlikely people and places. The ant and the king both seek love, but it is the ant who embodies the answer.

In the final section of this chapter, we invite you—the reader—to engage with the texts through personal reflection and collective action. This process allows the learning to move from cognition toward deeper recognition with yourself, the parables, and each other.

Some essential lessons to consider:

- Our worldview shapes our perception.
- Our reaction reveals our inner world.
- We are all short-sighted and have limited vision about something.
- The way to broaden our outlook is through listening, authentic communication, and beloved community.
- Through each other's perspectives, we can experience the world more completely.

Personal activity:

Inspired by the The Five Blind Men and The Elephant parable, take the time to answer these three questions:

> #1—"I am not completely certain," said the first man. "We should investigate." *Through a cultural lens, what do you do to learn about a different way of life?*
>
> #2 — "You are wrong," he said. "An elephant is not like a rope or a rug. Just like a pillar, it's high!" *Through a personal lens, when have you been mistaken about someone or something?*
>
> #3 — "They began to pound each other and yell." *Through an institutional lens, how does your affiliation with a particular political belief, position of power, or membership in a group inhibit your ability to listen to others?*

Collective practice:

For this exercise, find a partner to work with to explore each other's perspectives. If possible, sit across from one another, knee to knee and eye to eye. This activity has both a witness and a speaker. Meaning, you will both be part of the transformative practice.

Step 1: Choose who is going to be A and who is going to be B.
Step 2: Person A asks person B the first question repetitively.
First question: *Who are you?*

For example:
A: Who are you?
B: I am a daughter.
A: Who are you?
B: I am a singer.

Step 3: Continue to ask *Who are you?* for the next two minutes.
Step 4: Switch and repeat steps 1–3.
Step 5: Person B asks person A the second question repetitively. Second question: *Who do others think you are?*

Step 6: Continue to ask *Who do others think you are?* for the next two minutes.
Step 7: Switch and repeat.
Step 8: Person A asks person B the third question repetitively. Third question: *Who do you pretend to be?*
Step 9: Continue to ask *Who do you pretend to be?* for the next two minutes.
Step 10: Switch and repeat.

Summation: Spend five minutes having a conversation about what you heard and what you learned about each other. What were the commonalities, and what were the differences? Did you hit any walls? Did you have any breakthroughs?

We have provided guidance on *how* to use these stories to help us expand our perspectives. We have more in common than we might think. Yet self-absorbed projections affect our ability to see clearly.

> *I looked, and looked, and this I came to see:*
> *That what I thought was you and you,*
> *Was really me and me.*
> ~ Ancient Proverb ~[8]

The truth shines a bright light to reveal what's hidden and even illuminates the lies we tell ourselves about ourselves and others.

Notes

1. D. Meadows. (2000). *What Does It Mean to Be Human?* New York: St. Martin's Griffin, p. 68.
2. T. Merton, trans. (2010). *The Way of Chuang-Tzu.* New York: A New Directions Book, pp. 51–53.
3. H. Forest. (1996). *Wisdom Tales from Around the World.* Little Rock, AR: August House Publishers, pp. 25–26.
4. E. Davy Pearmain, ed. (2007). *Doorways to the Soul: 52 Wisdom Tales from Around the World.* Eugene, OR: Resource Publications, p. 280.
5. H. Forest. (1996). *Wisdom Tales from Around the World.* Little Rock, AR: August House Publishers, pp. 93–94.
6. H. Forest. (1996). *Wisdom Tales from Around the World.* Little Rock, AR: August House Publishers, pp. 42–43.
7. N. Khemir, comp. (1996). *The Wisdom of Islam,* story by Farid al-Din Attar, a Persian mystic poet. New York: Abbeville Press Publishers, p. 16.
8. K. Wilber. (2001). *No Boundary: Eastern and Western Approaches to Personal Growth.* Boston: Shambhala, p. 85.

6
THE JOURNEY INTO TRUTH

To tell the truth is to become beautiful, to begin to love yourself.
And that's political, in its most profound way.
~ June Jordan ~

Thus far we have traveled together along the path toward soulful awakening. We began this journey by turning our focus away from daily demands and peering into the still, silent space of our lives, between activities and thoughts. Letting go of doing, we created space for authentic *being* to arise. Breathing in and releasing out, our bodies quieted and relaxed; our minds opened and expanded. Leaning into this liberated space, we bent our ears to listen to the perspectives of others. Each one an invitation to consider alternative truths, hidden truths, more authentic truths—reflections into the mirror of our own inner reality. We have arrived at the doorway of our innermost being.
Shall we go in?

I have lived on the lip
of insanity, wanting to know reasons,
knocking on a door. It opens.
I've been knocking from the inside.
~ Rumi ~

Imagine Rumi's surprise when the door swings open from the inside. Without realizing it, his curiosity and search for understanding led him inward. The answers he sought were not outside of himself, in terms of books and facts, but were contained within the intimate library of his own life. What is true for Rumi is also true for us. The answers we seek are not outside of ourselves. We cannot purchase them; they cannot be given to us. We must fully and completely embody them.

So, let us commit and take another step forward on our journey—pivoting deeper down the path toward self-discovery.

The rhythm of this chapter is methodical. This is intentional. Although we knock on the door together, our entering is personal, even lonely. We're asking you to trust the process. The corridor that lies ahead leads into your inner library. Here, we hope you will experience Truth.

> *If you want to see the truth,*
> *You must be brave enough to look.*
> ~ Rune Lazulin ~

The way forward may at first appear dark, as this is unchartered territory. No need to worry; your eyes will adjust. As you move inward, you will be met by sages. These guides from disparate traditions have already walked and talked inside these very same walls. In their search for truth, they left a flickering light—a story lamp—illuminating the way. As you progress along this path into truth, pay close attention to their insights; listen, question, and ponder the wisdom these elders have to share. When you finally emerge from the library of your life, you will have a bit more clarity, and the light inside your soul will twinkle a bit brighter.

The first lamp—Commit to the search.

> *If you are searching,*
> *You must not stop until you find.*
> *When you find, however,*
> *You will become troubled.*
> *Your confusion will give way to wonder.*
> *In wonder you will reign over all things.*
> *Your sovereignty will be your rest.*
> ~ Gospel of Thomas ~

Real seeking is driven by deep curiosity, a want to find. What does it take to move from a seeker to a finder? *The Gospel of Thomas* describes the work of authentic being and becoming. Thomas outlines that the quest begins within—in the pure desire to know. These questions (like Rumi wanting to know the reasons) will lead you through the labyrinth of the unknown to the known, from many truths to Truth. It's intense. It is not a quest for the faint of heart. The search into the territories of interiority often creates disturbance but persevere on this quest for self-awareness is a manifestation of your own divine purpose.

> *If you look for the truth outside yourself,*
> *It gets farther and farther away.*
> ~ Tung-Shan ~

Take a moment to ponder: What Truth am I searching for? _____
_____

The second lamp—Truth resides within.

A commitment to finding Truth, leads to the second lamp. Too often, answers are sought in the well-lit places, among the familiar and acceptable. But is this where the ultimate Truth hides? Listen to *The Lost Jewel*, which has numerous iterations throughout various cultures and underscores the importance of place—the *where*. It's a reminder that the treasured Truth is found in the concealed spaces deep within our own hearts. The quest is to find and reveal the lost jewel.

The Lost Jewel

There once was a woman who was looking for her lost jewels in the village square. The other villagers wished her well and were trying to help her find this treasure in the area in and around the square. They had been searching fruitlessly for some time, when someone asked her: "But exactly where did you lose this treasure?"

"I lost it in my home," the woman answered.

"But are you crazy? If you lost it in your home, why are you having us help you search out here in the square?"

"And you, my friend," she replied, "is this not what you are always doing, searching for your treasure in the streets, in the square, when it is really in your own home that you lost what you most want? Don't you go everywhere in vain search of peace and happiness, your greatest treasure, which you have lost in your own home? In your own heart—that is where you must search. It is there that your treasure has always been waiting to be found."[1]

Let's ponder this story about a lost jewel. Although there were many people engaged in the search for it, they were all looking in the wrong place. Thus, the time and effort spent searching, although well-intended, was futile. It never was in the village square, so how could it possibly be found there? The search needed redirection. The jewel was lost in the woman's home and therefore, could only be found there. Similarly, our jewel of Truth lies in wait within. As the *Gospel of Matthew* asserts, "For where your treasure is, there also will your heart be" (6:21).

What prevents you from seeking Truth within? _____
_____
_____

The third lamp—Discern truth.

There are cautionary tales told within many wisdom traditions that highlight the importance of discerning truth. Take, for example, the three tales presented next, one from ancient Greece, one from Ethiopia, and the other from India. The first story depicts the uncanny resemblance between truth and falsehood that is only surmised upon closer inspection. The second story explores the cunning nature of falsehood and the enduring battle to reveal truth. And the third story reminds us that we must discern the truth no matter what the cost.

What is considered to be truth, could be a trick:

Veritas

Prometheus, the potter, decided to sculpt the form of Veritas (Truth), using all his skill so that she would be able to regulate people's behavior. As he was working, an unexpected summons from mighty Jupiter called him away. Prometheus left cunning Dolus (Trickery) in charge of his workshop (Dolus had recently become one of the god's apprentices). Dolus used the time at his disposal to fashion with his sly fingers a figure of the same size and appearance as Veritas with identical features. When he had almost completed the piece, which was truly remarkable, he ran out of clay to use for her feet.

The master returned, so Dolus quickly sat down in his seat, quaking with fear. Prometheus was amazed at the similarity of the two statues and wanted it to seem as if all the credit were due to his own skill. Therefore, he put both statues in the kiln and when they had been thoroughly baked, he infused them both with life: sacred Veritas walked with measured steps, while her unfinished twin stood stuck in her tracks.

That forgery, that product of subterfuge, thus acquired the name of Mendacium [Falsehood], and I readily agree with people who say that she has no feet: every once in a while, something that is false can start off successfully, but with time Veritas (Truth) is sure to prevail.[2]

Although both statues had identical features and were infused with life, only one had "measured steps." It is a small but significant distinction. Truth has the ability and power to walk forth—to go out into the world with regulated conduct—whereas falsehood (her twin) cannot. Since they look astonishingly alike, their difference must be discerned through embodied actions. As James Baldwin teaches, "I can't believe what you say, because I see what you do."

Now, let's engage with another story. This one is from ancient Ethiopia.

Fire, Water, Truth and Falsehood

Fire, Water, Truth and Falsehood

Long ago, Fire, Water, Truth, and Falsehood lived together in one large house. Although all were polite toward each other, they kept their distance. Truth and Falsehood sat on opposite sides of the room. Fire constantly leapt out of Water's path.

One day they went hunting together. They found a large number of cattle and began driving them home to their village. "Let us share these cattle equally," said Truth as they traveled across the grasslands. "This is the fair way to divide our captives."

No one disagreed with Truth except Falsehood. Falsehood wanted more than an equal share but kept quiet about it for the moment. As the four hunters traveled back to the village, Falsehood went secretly to Water and whispered, "You are more powerful than Fire. Destroy Fire and then there will be more cattle for each of us!"

Water flowed over Fire, bubbling and steaming until Fire was gone. Water meandered along, cheerfully thinking about more cattle for itself.

Falsehood, meanwhile, whispered to Truth. "Look! See for yourself! Water has killed Fire! Let us leave Water, who has cruelly destroyed our warmhearted friend. We must take the cattle high in the mountains to graze."

As Truth and Falsehood traveled up the mountain, Water tried to follow. But the mountain was too steep, and Water could not flow upwards. Water washed down upon itself, splashing and swirling around rocks as it tumbled down the slope. Look and see! Water is still tumbling down the mountainside to this day.

Truth and Falsehood arrived at the mountaintop. Falsehood turned to Truth and said in a loud voice, "I am more powerful than you! You will be my servant. I am your master. All the cattle belong to me!"

Truth rose up and spoke out, "I will not be your servant!"

They battled and battled. Finally, they brought the argument to Wind to decide who was master.

Wind didn't know. Wind blew all over the world to ask people whether Truth or Falsehood was more powerful. Some people said, "A single word of Falsehood can completely destroy Truth." Others insisted, "Like a small candle in the dark, Truth can change every situation."

Wind finally returned to the mountain and said, "I have seen that Falsehood is very powerful. But it can rule only where Truth has stopped struggling to be heard."

And it has been that way ever since.[3]

The natural elements of the world help us learn and discern how to find truth. This particular tale demonstrates that truth is a battleground, discovered through the struggles to live honestly. The more we light the candle of truth within ourselves, the more the mirage and power of falsehood diminishes.

Justice yearns for truth.

The Buddhist tradition also sheds light on the importance of discerning truth. In the Buddhist monastic lineage, children were selected at an early age to live in a monastery with their teachers. Based on this tradition, whatever the elder monks asked, the younger monks were obliged to do. These teachers were often held in high regard, deemed wise and just.

Notice the power dynamics in this next story and the logic and courage of one of the students.

The Wise Master

There was once a teacher who lived with a great number of students in a run-down temple. The students supported themselves by begging for food in the bustling streets of a nearby town. Some of the students grumbled about their humble living conditions. In response, the old master said one day, "We must repair the walls of this temple. Since we occupy ourselves with study and meditation, there is no time to earn the money we will need. I have thought of a simple solution."

All the students eagerly gathered closer to hear the words of their teacher. The Master said, "Each of you must go into the town and steal goods that can be sold for money. In this way, we will be able to do the good work of repairing our temple."

The students were startled at this suggestion from the wise master. But since they respected him greatly, they assumed he must have good judgment and did not protest.

The wise master said sternly, "In order not to defile our excellent reputation by committing illegal and immoral acts, please be certain to steal when no one is looking. I do not want anyone to be caught."

When the teacher walked away, the students discussed the plan among themselves. "It is wrong to steal," said one. "Why has our wise master asked us to do this?" Another retorted, "It will allow us to build our temple, which is a good result." They all agreed that their teacher was wise and just and must have a sensible reason for making such an unusual request. They set out eagerly for the town, promising each other that they would not disgrace their school by getting caught. "Be careful," they called to one another. "Do not let anyone see you stealing."

All the students except one young boy set forth. The wise master approached him and asked, "Why do you stay behind?"

The boy responded, "I cannot follow your instructions to steal where no one will see me. Wherever I go, I am always there watching. My own eyes will see me steal."

The wise master tearfully embraced the boy. "I was just testing the integrity of my students," he said. "You are the only one who has passed the test!"

The boy went on to become a great teacher himself.[4]

What an unusual request, thought the young monks, and so they began to discern what was being asked of them. However, in their discernment process, they acquiesced their truth to the authority of their teacher. The teacher was deemed the sovereign one. Although they knew stealing was wrong, they began to justify it, thereby losing their own integrity. That is, all but one young monk, who held to his truth. As a student and seeker aware of his "own eyes watching," he discovered his sovereignty and became an authentic guide for others.

Cover not truth with falsehood, nor conceal the truth when you know what it is.
~ The Holy Qur'an ~

There are a lot of mirages and false narratives that can deter us from reaching Truth. This can be found not only in spiritual traditions but within political, racial, educational, and cultural ones as well. Sometimes we get so inspired by someone else's teachings or personality traits that we forget to look within. It's like trying to use someone else's fingerprint to unlock your cellphone. It just won't work. As learners on a quest, we are challenged to recognize the difference between what is true and untrue, real and unreal throughout our lives. This is an essential part of the journey toward sovereignty.

What prevents you from discerning truth? Where have you been tricked into a falsehood? _____

_____

So far, we have listened to various sages share their wisdom, all pointing to the fact that truth lies within us. Our work is to discern truth as we can be easily misled, whether by others who claim to be our teachers and guides or by our own intimate fears and desires. Therefore, let us persevere and press onward.

Knowing yourself is the key, but being true to yourself is what turns it, opening the door to reveal a world of joy and delight.[5]

The fourth lamp—Holding fast to Truth.

We have reached another lamp burning brightly along our interior corridor, its light revealing that the virtues we work to cultivate all exist along a single thread deep within us. In the forthcoming story, *An Ancient Myth*, what is the main virtue, and how does it connect to the others?

An Ancient Myth

A king once invited merchants from all over the region to attend a big craft fair, assuring each that he would purchase whatever did not sell. One blacksmith of limited intelligence brought an iron image of Saturn to the fair, and since no one purchased it, the king's officers procured it and delivered it to his majesty. That night in a dream, the king saw a luminous female form—obviously a goddess—leaving his body. "Who are you?" he asked in some alarm. "I am Lakshmi, goddess of wealth and prosperity," the figure replied. "I cannot remain in the same place where Saturn remains." The king saluted her respectfully but allowed her to depart.

Next emerged a male deity, Glory (vaibhava) who cannot remain with anyone who has no prosperity. The king allowed him to go as well. They departed in order: Righteousness (dharma), Stauchness (dhairya), Compassion (daya), Forbearance (kshama), and a host of other virtues, but when Truthfulness (satya) prepared to leave, the king grabbed his feet and would not let him go saying, "I've never left you all these years, and you cannot leave me now."

All the other good qualities had been waiting outside the door for Truth to emerge, that they might all seek shelter elsewhere. When he did not appear after quite a long time, Righteousness finally said, "I have to go back; I cannot exist without Truth," and so he returned. He was followed by all the others, in reverse order from their departure, and at last even Lakshmi returned, telling the king, "It is thanks to your love of Truth that you have all of us back; we could not resist. A fellow like you who holds to Truth won't ever be miserable.[6]

In the celestial stories of India, Saturn is often portrayed as a powerful force that can alter one's life. As the remover of fortunes, no one wants to be under Saturn's influence. This is precisely why the statue of Saturn was not purchased at the craft fair. Who wants to lose wealth, recognition, and fame? Yet, Saturn teaches a profound spiritual lesson. Notice where the virtues originated. They emerged from within the king because he had already nurtured and embodied them within himself. Saturn challenges us to cultivate Truth and hold fast to it, to let go of all falsehoods and allow Truth to be the center of our lives.

Be a Truth-seeker. The story above reminds us to hold fast to Truth and this next instruction, from Buddha to his disciple Ananda, shows us the solitary nature of this work:

A Lamp unto Yourself

Therefore Ananda, be ye lamps unto yourselves, be ye a refuge to yourselves. Betake yourselves to no external refuge. Hold fast to the Truth as a lamp; hold fast to the Truth as a refuge. Look not for a refuge in anyone besides yourselves. And those, Ananda, who either now or after I am dead shall be a lamp unto themselves, shall betake themselves to no external refuge, but holding fast to the Truth as their lamps, and holding fast to the Truth as their refuge, shall not look for refuge to anyone beside themselves—it is they who shall reach the very topmost Height. But they must be anxious to learn.[7]

How do you hold firmly to Truth? _____
_____

Ignorance *is* bliss. Enlightenment *is* work. It's possible to live our entire lives and never know Truth. In this world of 24-hour everything (television, entertainment, social media, shopping), we are easily pulled outside ourselves to seek our treasures externally. We seek power, status, and wealth but what about Truth? How much time do we spend seeking Truth? As an elder once shared, "Don't die with the song still inside you." Bring it forth and sing.

What truth do you need to bring forth and sing? _____
_____
_____

The fifth lamp—Truth as subject.

We want to emphasize and explain a distinction here between objective and subjective truth. Objective truth can be measured and quantified. It is the number of pages in this book, the height of a person, the circumference of the earth. Take, for instance, the story *The Blind Men and the Elephant* (presented in the previous chapter): the elephant can be weighed and measured, but do these measurements encompass the whole of the elephant? No, because these are only objective truths *about* the elephant. Valid in terms of the exterior dimension, but still incomplete because it misses the interior dimension of the elephant (the subject). Each fact can be accurate yet lack the ultimate Truth of the elephant's entirety.

Subjective truth is alive; it is connected to our individual soul and the collective soul of the world. As the story notes, "The elephant stood, quite undefined, in the garden of ancient past." All the measurements in the world and all the comparisons to what the elephant is like missed the subjective truth of the elephant as a living being. Confucius gives words to the total symbiotic relationship between beingness and Truth.

> *Truth does not depart from human nature.*
> *If what is regarded as truth departs from human nature,*
> *it may not be regarded as truth.*
> ~ Confucius ~

It is this subjective truth within human nature that we seek; therefore, we must continue inward. As Laude notes, "The truth is that which cannot be utterly forgotten, although it may be veiled or concealed, and even temporarily put out of mind, because it is our very consciousness, or rather Consciousness itself."[8]

The sixth lamp—Truth is the ultimate manifestation of who you are.

The Upanishads, ancient texts from India, share various dialogues between truth seekers and sages engaged in self-inquiry. *Who am I?* To the surprise of many, these truth seekers discover that they are the Truth they seek. Truth *is* the core, nature and essence of their being, described as *Sat-Chit-Ananda* (Truth-Consciousness-Bliss).[9] Truth is being, and being is Truth. There is a sacred oneness to this unity. As you become conscious of this alignment, you experience the totality of your own being as a blissful radiation.

How do you bring truth, consciousness, and bliss into alignment? Jesus offers an answer. In the *Gospel of John*, Jesus said to his disciples, "Very truly, I tell you, before Abraham was, I am." This "I am" statement is a significant teaching,

"I am the way, the truth and the light."[10] From one perspective, Jesus is saying *he* is the way, the truth and the light, yet there is another perspective to consider. What if Jesus is drawing his disciple's attention to look deeper into themselves, to center themselves in the "I AM."[11] Take a breath into the "I AM." Rest in the infinite power of "I AM" and listen to "the still small voice" of the Spirit inside of you.[12]

During the 9th century, Husayn ibn Mansur al-Hallaj (a Sufi master from Baghdad) received such a blissful experience of Truth that he ran into the marketplace shouting, "*ana l'haq*" (I am Truth). His profound realization that he and Truth are one led him to teach about the *inner hajj*, the sacred journey to the abode of Allah found within one's own heart.

So many sages from diverse times and traditions turn us inward because they each discovered that Truth *is* the essence of being; it is integrity, pure authenticity, and sovereignty.

Who am I? This honest repetitive inquiry propels us forward into the sacred book of Self. Who am I is a ritual. A meditation on being true.

Who am I? _____
Who am I? _____
Who am I? _____

When will I ever see that Am that I Am?
~ Rumi ~

The seventh lamp—Truth is revolutionary.

The journey toward truth disposes and deposes falsehoods. As the saying goes, "Tell the Truth and shame the devil." No longer surrendering to the demands of the false self (e.g., money, power, status); no longer swayed and manipulated by external factors (political, social, and material motives); no longer bowing to praise, power, and position, *I revolt*. I turn within.

Truth shines as itself
in your imageless mind,
It is self-sustaining light,
And whoever partakes of it
Does so only in the imageless mind,
Allowing you to see beyond
The delusion and fog of temporary mind.[13]

To wake up requires traversing the inner terrain into the deeper Truth of who you are. Through this cycle, older thoughts fade away, revealing a truer, more illuminated self. This is revolutionary (Latin *revolvere*); it's a conscious choice to change direction. In so doing, truth becomes an inner movement. It is not only a revolutionary act; it is *the* revolutionary act. *I am* the re-evolution.

As Mahatma Gandhi stated,

> All the tendencies present in the outer world are to be found in the world of our body. If we could change ourselves, the tendencies in the world would also change. As a man [woman] changes his [her] own nature, so does the attitude of the world change towards him [her]. This is the divine mystery supreme. A wonderful thing it is and the source of our happiness. We need not wait to see what others do.[14]

As you stand in your own truth, you serve as a light to others. This is how we transform. As the Sacramento poet Dre-T teaches, "Courage is contagious, just like fear."

We began this chapter by entering the womb-like corridors of our inner world to discover Truth. We listened to the words of the lamplighters and considered them in the midst of our own lived experiences.

The doors of the library are before you; are you knocking on your inner door? What's inside? _____

_____

Truth-seeking is a struggle, yet it's a beautiful struggle. The below old Black spiritual reminds us that on the other side of the door is the essence—not just the essence of ourselves but of each other.

> *Rock-a my soul in the bosom of Abraham*
> *Rock-a my soul in the bosom of Abraham*
> *Rock-a my soul in the bosom of Abraham*
> *Oh! Rock-a my soul.*
> *So high! You can't get over it.*
> *So low! You can't get under it.*
> *So wide! You can't get around it.*
> *You've got to go in through the door!*

May we not die with our sacred song still hidden away and locked inside. Let it out. Let it live. Let it breathe. Let it be.

It's time to sing!

Can you feel it? You've actually arrived inside your inner library and realized you are the book of Truth. Let Truth out and let Truth shine. It's time to wake up!

It's time to dance!

The seven lamps illuminating Truth:

1. Commit to the search.
2. Truth resides within.
3. Discern truth.
4. Hold fast to truth.
5. Truth as subject.
6. Truth is who we are.
7. Truth is revolutionary.

Questions for deeper inquiry:

- Why is the search for truth important?
- What truth am I searching for?
- Where am I searching for truth?
- How am I discerning truth from falsehood in my daily life?
- What internal truth do I need to share and sing with the world?

Personal practice:

Find a place to sit quietly. Repeat this stanza three times: *I am the key.* Now, ask yourself, "Who am I?" Listen to the responses. Write down what arises.

I am _____.

I am not _____.

Then ask yourself, do any of these responses actually get to the core nature of who *I AM*? Not what you are but *who* you are.

Collective practice:

Choose one of the stories or quotes from this chapter. Read slowly and silently through the ritual of *lectio divina*.[15] Take time with it. Chew, savor, and chant the words as a way to extract their essence.

- What word or line speaks to you? Explain.
- How does this word or line speak to you in regard to your search for truth?
- What would you like to know more about?
- Does this story relate to your own experience? Why or Why not?

Write your thoughts down. Now bring your ideas from your personal process into the collective circle of discovery.

_____
_____
_____

With great truth comes great responsibility. There will be peaks and valleys, treachery and triumph. Yet truth is that lamp that shines eternally—light upon light—burning with love.

> *If we're gonna heal,*
> *let it be glorious.*
> ~ Warsan Shire ~

Notes

1. This ancient story, versions of which are found in many oral traditions, is from J. Leloup. (2002). *The Gospel of Mary Magdalene*. Rochester, VT: Inner Traditions, p. 69.
2. Aesop Fables 530 (from Phaedrus Appendix 5). www.theoi.com/Daimon/Dolos.html.
3. H. Forest. (1996). *Wisdom Tales from Around the World*. Little Rock, AK: August House Publishers, p. 91.
4. H. Forest. (1996). *Wisdom Tales from Around the World*. Little Rock, AK: August House Publishers, pp. 15–16.
5. Poor Richards Almanac. https://ourfriendben.wordpress.com/2008/05/04/to-thine-own-self-be-true.
6. R. Svoboda. (1997). *The Greatness of Saturn*. Hyderabad: Sadhana Publications, pp. 254–255.
7. T. W. Rhys-Davids, trans. (2007). "The Mahaparinibbana Sutta." In *The Teachings of the Buddha*, ed. J. Kornfield. Boston: Shambhala, p. 125.
8. P. Laude. (2011–2012). "The Truth of Truths." *Parabola*, 35, Winter.
9. For more information on The Upanishads see E. Easwaran, trans. (2007). *The Upanishads*. Tomales, CA: Nilgiri Press.
10. *The Gospel of John*, 8: 58; 14:6.
11. According to K. Wilbur. (2017). *The Religion of Tomorrow*. Boston: Shambhala, p. 117, "This pure I AMness is the deep, clear Awareness in you that right now is simply, spontaneously, and effortlessly Witnessing all that is arising-this page, this computer, this room, this landscape-and yet it is identified with none of it: 'neti, neti' 'I AM not this, not that, but rather its simple Witness.' This I AMness, this Witness, this silent, clear, Observing Self realizes that 'I have sensations of those objects; I have sensations, but I am not those sensations, I have feelings, but I am not those feelings, I have thoughts, but I am not those thoughts.'"
12. *The book of Psalms*, Psalm 46:10.
13. *Dharmakaya Sutra* 4.12 in R. Shapiro, ed. (2017). *The World Wisdom Bible: A New Testament for Global Spirituality*. Woodstock, VT: Skylight Path Publishing, p. 31.
14. https://josephranseth.com/gandhi-didnt-say-be-the-change-you-want-to-see-in-the-world.
15. *Lectio divina* is a contemplative practice of listening to, discerning, and responding to a text. For more on *lectio divina*, see M. Keator. (2018). *Lectio Divina as Contemplative Pedagogy: Reappropriating Monastic Practice for the Humanities*. London: Routledge; M. Keator. (2019). "Writing About Yoga: Lectio Divina and the Awakening of the Soul." In *The Whole Person: Embodying Teaching and Learning Through Lectio and Visio Divina*. New York: Rowman & Littlefield.

7
INTO THE HEART OF HEALING

<u>Pain</u>

And a woman spoke, saying, Tell us of Pain.
And he said,
Your pain is the breaking of the shell
that encloses your understanding.

Even as the stone of the fruit must break,
That its heart may stand in the sun, so must
You know pain.

And could you keep your heart in wonder
At the daily miracles of life, your pain would not
seem less wonderous than your Joy;

And you would accept the seasons of your
heart, even as you have always accepted
The seasons that pass over your fields.
And you would watch with serenity
Through the winters of your grief.

Much of your pain is self-chosen.
It is the bitter potion by which the
physician within you heals your sick self.

Therefore, trust the physician, and drink
His remedy in silence and tranquility.

For his hand, though heavy and hard, is
guided by the tender hand of the Unseen.

And the cup he brings, though it burn your lips,
has been fashioned of the clay
which the Potter has moistened with His
own sacred tears.
~ Kahlil Gibran ~[1]

No one likes to suffer. It is uncomfortable and traumatic. But in truth, no one escapes suffering. Perhaps instead of running from it, we can sit in it and listen to it. What then does our pain teach?

The Guest House

This being human is a guest house.
Every morning a new arrival.
A joy, a depression, a meanness,
some momentary awareness comes
as an unexpected visitor.
Welcome and entertain them all!
Even if they are a crowd of sorrows,
who violently sweep your house
empty of its furniture,
still, treat each guest honorably.
He may be clearing you out
for some new delight.
The dark thought, the shame, the malice.
Meet them at the door laughing and invite them in.
Be grateful for whatever comes.
Because each has been sent
as a guide from beyond.
~ Rumi ~[2]

If all of these different feelings are in fact life's greatest teachers, this changes our relationship to them. It is not about sweeping things under the rug or pushing them down or denying their existence. It is not about looking away. No! Take the deep dive into the well and welcome *all* that is inside your heart.

Heart Breaks

The pupil comes to the rebbe[3] and asks,
"Why does Torah tell us to 'place these words *upon* your hearts?
Why does it not tell us to place these holy words *in* our hearts?

The rebbe answers,
"It is because as we are, our hearts are closed,
and we cannot place the holy words in our hearts.

So we place them on top of our hearts.
And there they stay, until one day,
the heart breaks, and the words fall in."[4]

The breaking open of the heart for love and deeper healing, has a sacred purpose. But, damn, it is painful. The truth is, we are birthed in and through pain. Pain is powerful. Pain creates an opportunity for growth and presents a potential for something greater to arise.

<u>Japanese Bowl</u>

I'm like one of those Japanese bowls
That were made long ago
I have some cracks in me
They have been filled with gold
That's what they used back then
When they had a bowl to mend

It did not hide the cracks
It made them shine instead

So now every old scar shows
From every time I broke
And anyone's eyes can see
I'm not what I used to be

But in a collector's mind
All of these jagged lines
Make me more beautiful
And worth a much higher price

I'm like one of those Japanese bowls
I was made long ago
I have some cracks you can see
See how they shine of gold.[5]

Just like the Japanese bowls, we are filled with jagged lines and broken pieces. When something is broken and has suffered damage, it has a history. Our experiences can make us even more beautiful.

The wound is the place the Light enters you.
~Rumi ~

Take a moment to answer the following questions:
Where do you hold pain in your body? _____
_____.
Why does it live there? _____
_____.
Who introduced you to this pain? _____
_____.
How do you release the pain from having a hold on you? _____
_____.

Place this anthem *onto* your heart. Let it sit there and sing. Can you hear the offering?

Anthem

Ring the bells that still can ring
Forget your perfect offering
There is a crack, a crack in everything
That's how the light gets in.
~ Leonard Cohen ~

The rhythm of healing pulses through the heart. There is a language of the heart. Interpreting this language requires being in tune and attuned to your own wounds and needs.

Our hearts sing many songs. For example, in the *Psalms of David*, he sings about war and grief, hope and love. Singing releases the emotions of the heart and creates new alignment. Rise and show yourself. I'm listening. Sing yourself into being.

What does it mean to chant and sing, speak and pray from the heart space?

_____

The song of my heart is _____.

To turn any of our pains into power takes almighty hard heart work. Break open your heart because it is in the breaking that the heart finds its wings. It is in the falling in love that we learn to fly.

The path into the heart of healing is not paved with shame or blame. It is not a path of judgement or even guilt, which can turn hearts into heavy weights that drown us in our sorrows. We can't think our way out of pain; we have to surrender to it. We have to face it, name it, and sing it.

We can't fix our broken hearts, but we can be transformed through them, just like the Japanese bowl. Radical vulnerability pushes us to be present to the strengthening of the heart.

Let the heart cry out.
Let the heart break.
Let the heart break open.
Trust Truth.
Healing is near.
In the abode of the heart.
Love is salve; love is balm.
Love is life.
Only a heart can heal another heart.
That's how healed people, heal people.
The power of the heart is clear.
Love is the medicine.
~ Mary and Vajra ~

The Dance of the Soul

I have loved in life and I have been loved.
I have drunk the bowl of poison
from the hands of love as nectar, and
have been raised above life's joy and sorrow.

> My heart, aflame in love, set afire every
> heart that came in touch with it.
> My heart has been rent and joined again;
> My heart has been broken and again made whole;
>
> My heart has been wounded and healed again;
> A thousand deaths my heart has died, and
> thanks be to love, it lives yet.
>
> I went through hell and saw there
> love's raging fire, and I entered heaven illuminated
> with the light of love.
>
> I wept in love and made all weep with me;
> I mourned in love and pierced the hearts of men;
> And when my fiery glance fell on the rocks,
> the rocks burst forth as volcanoes.
>
> The whole world sank in the flood caused by my one tear;
> With my deep sigh the earth trembled, and
> when I cried aloud the name of my beloved,
> I shook the throne of God in heaven.
>
> I bowed my head low in humility, and
> On my knees I begged of love,
> "Disclose to me, I pray thee, O love, thy secret."
>
> She took me gently by my arms and lifted me
> above the earth, and spoke softly in my ear,
> "My dear one, thou thyself art love, art lover,
> and thyself art the beloved whom thou hast adored."
> ~ Hazrat Inayat Khan ~

A mystical description of becoming one. A dancing of the soul inside the heartbeat of creation.

Love is a divine relationship that is ever-present and eternal. It is absolutely everything over and over again. The love, lover, and beloved are within, calling and connecting us. These bridges are intergenerational, and often sacred lessons are passed between teacher and student. Another layer to notice. Hazrat Inayat Khan was the teacher of Murshid Sam. Next is Sam's iteration of the wisdom he learned from his Sufi guide.

The Bowl of Saki

The heart is not living until it has experienced pain.
The angel lives in the heart-sphere but does not know pain.
There is a lack of strength in the love.
This is something like the natural love of the infant.
It is only when love is tested that love can show its strength.
If it turns to hate or any emotion, that shows there was no life.
Sufis are able to experience pain in the heart
without being drowned by it.
~ Murshid Sam L. Lewis ~[6]

Too often, we hold ourselves and others as fragile porcelain. Yet suffering is a part of life. Sometimes we just need to let go and allow bits and pieces of ourselves to break open and fall away. Our pain may be trying to heal something. Or it may be drawing out a deeper picture that moves us toward greater belonging and wholeness. It is both revealing and revelatory. As Rumi shared, it "may be clearing you out for some new delight." From this perspective, we can begin to see suffering as a living lesson guiding us.

What have you learned through a painful experience? _____
_____
_____

Is it possible to love someone back into existence? Why or why not?
_____
_____
_____
_____

Cynthia Bourgeault (2008) reminds us,

> When we mourn, we are in a state of freefall, our heart reaching out toward what we seemingly lost but cannot help love anyway . . . Mourning is a brutal form of emptiness. But in this emptiness, if we can remain open, we discover that a mysterious "something" does indeed reach back to comfort us; the tendrils of our grief trailing out into the unknown become intertwined in a greater love that holds all things together.[7]

Let your spiritual self hold your human self. Hear this personal testimony from Mary that takes us into an intimate moment of rest and release. Pain was emerging and diffusing in this no-time-space of surrender. Energy depleted. Agendas gone. Her journal entry is below:

> Yesterday, my human self was exhausted. I had a horrible headache. Utterly drained from the recent death of my dad, family pains and struggles, the ongoing isolation, and almost a year of teaching online. I cocooned myself into my old green cotton sleeping bag. I rested there on the floor allowing my sorrow and heartache to flow. A perfect storm arising. In the midst of it all, I could sense my higher self, my spiritual self there. She was quiet, but present. Without judging me, assessing me or trying to fix me, she held space for me to move through my process. For nine hours. There was no pushing or rushing. All was calm and gentle as I wept and rested.
> —Mary, February 19, 2021

Sometimes the solution is found *within* the cocoon.

Many of us are enamored with the beauty of the butterfly. However, let's consider the power of the cocoon. Throughout our lives, our cocoons come in so many different forms. Cocoons can represent moments of trial, tribulation, isolation, and even tremendous growth. Whether the cocoon is physical, mental, or metaphorical, there's a lesson there.

The Struggle of the Butterfly

A man found a cocoon of a butterfly. He sat and watched the butterfly for several hours as it struggled to force its body through the little hole at the end. Eventually, the butterfly stopped making progress. It appeared as if it had gotten as far as it could and it could go no farther. The man decided to help the butterfly, so he took a pair of scissors and snipped off the remaining bit of the cocoon. The butterfly then emerged easily, but it had a swollen body and small, shriveled wings.

The man continued to watch the butterfly because he expected that, at any moment, the wings would enlarge and expand to be able to support the body, which would contract in time. Neither happened! In fact, the butterfly spent the rest of its life crawling around with a swollen body and shriveled wings.

It never was able to fly.

What the man in his kindness and haste did not understand was that the restricting cocoon and the struggle required for the butterfly to get through the tiny opening were nature's way of forcing fluid from the body of the butterfly into its wings, so that it would be ready for flight once it achieved its freedom from the cocoon.

Sometimes struggles are exactly what we need in our life. If nature allowed us to go through our life without any obstacles, it would cripple us. We would not be as strong as what we could have been. And we could never fly.[8]

The man above was kind but lacked the patience and faith in the process of nature. We've all been there! We get into trouble when we tie transformation to a clock, deadline, or deliverable. But delivery doesn't work like that—without reaching our breaking point, we do not break open. It's in breaking open that we break free.

We've got to get on butterfly time. Butterflies are revered in different traditions—from the Aztecs to the Hindus to the Greeks. Although these places are seemingly different, in each of them, the butterfly is a metaphor for the soul.

```
We delight in the beauty of the butterfly, but
rarely admit the changes it has gone through to
              achieve that beauty.

                  ~Maya Angelou
```

```
Out of suffering have emerged the
strongest souls; the most massive
characters are seared with scars.

                    ~Kahlil Gibran
```

```
you do not have to be a fire for
   every mountain blocking you.
         you could be a water
and soft river your way to freedom
                              too.

                        ~options
              Nayirrah Waheed, SALT
```

Butterflies do not know borders. They fly over walls. They are not bound by the earth. Have you heard of the butterfly effect? That a butterfly can flap its wings in San Antonio, Texas, and cause a tornado half-way around the world? There is also the butterfly effect of kindness, healing, and world peace.

I'm capable of anything, my imagination could give me wings
To fly like doves over the streets watchin' many things
Kids walkin home from school, on drug blocks, missionaries
Pass out papers that read love god
I see faces cases, judges n jurors, masons lawyers n cops
I watch 'cause every thug's face is my mirror.
~ Nas ~

Even the butterfly has to land. Place matters. How we grew up and where we are now impact who we are.

Grandfather
Sacred one,
Look at our brokenness.
We know that in all creation
Only the human family
Has strayed from the Sacred Way.

We know that we are the ones
Who are divided.
And we are the ones
Who must come back together
To walk in the Sacred Way.

Grandfather
Sacred one,
Teach us love, compassion, and honor
That we may heal the earth
And heal each other.

My words are tied in one
With the great mountains
With the great rocks,
With the great trees,
In one with my body
And my heart.

Do you all help me
With supernatural power,
And you day,
And you, night!
All of you see me
One with this world!
~ Prayer of the Chippewa/Ojibway Anishinabe Nation ~[9]

All of the world is alive: one body, one heart, one love. To walk in the sacred way is to become one with these symbiotic interconnections. Without pain, we do not know joy. Without earth, we do not know sky. Our words are tied to the great mountains. The great tree of knowledge grows our wisdom. Imagine that! There is no separation in the healing.

One way we can begin to heal is to reconnect to the earth's energies.

*When you realize HEART and EARTH are spelled
with the same letters, it all starts to make sense.*
~ Jennifer Bramley ~

Of all the classrooms in the world, the earth teaches us balance, interdependence, and harmony.

Ute Prayer

Earth, teach me quiet as the grasses are still with new light.
Earth, teach me suffering as old stones suffer with memory.
Earth, teach me humility as blossoms are humble with beginning.
Earth, teach me caring as mothers nurture their young.
Earth, teach me courage as the tree that stands alone.
Earth, teach me limitation as the ant that crawls on the ground.
Earth, teach me freedom as the eagle that soars in the sky.
Earth, teach me acceptance as the leaves that die each fall.
Earth, teach me renewal as the seed that rises in the spring.
Earth, teach me to forget myself as melted snow forgets its life.
Earth, teach me to remember kindness as dry fields weep with rain.[10]

The heart of healing and the heart of teaching echo each other. If we, ourselves, are forces of nature, then how can we magnify one another *through* education?

Our answer is to bring the sacred into schooling. But to do so, we have to tease apart the differences between teaching as profession and teaching as transgression (hooks, 1994), between the institution of schooling and the nature of learning, between oppression and education, between the world (as constructed today) and Mother Earth (who is completely natural). Essentially, we have to tap into a different source. Change the lineage, alter the axiology. When earth becomes our common lineage, our entire foundation shifts.

Axis of Energy

Travel with us into a somewhat esoteric space to locate magnetic pedagogy.

> *Our entire biological system,*
> *the brain and the earth itself,*
> *work on the same frequencies.*
> ~ Nikola Tesla ~

We are in fact, earthlings: "The Lord God formed Adam from the soil of the ground and breathed into his nostrils the breath of life, and the man became a living being" (Genesis 2:7).[11] Adam comes from the Hebrew word *Adamah*, meaning living soil. From the beginnings of time, living beings lived in an intimate symbiotic relationship to the earth. As living beings of the living soil, we are also electromagnetic energies (consider the chakra system). In fact, both our brain and heart radiate electro-magnetic fields. Yet our strongest force of energy comes from the electro-magnetic field of our heart.[12]

The Earth also consists of electro-magnetic fields. In fact, the Earth is like a giant battery that continues to regenerate itself through the continuous flow

The Earth's Magnetic Field

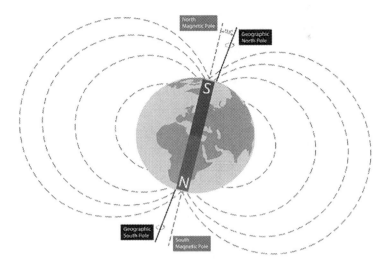

between its core and the skies (solar radiation and lightening). This renewing energy flow is known as a torus field. See illustration above.

The earth's magnetic field makes a compass work. But not only do human beings rely on the earth's magnetic fields, according to *Nature Communications*,[13] butterflies also use magnetic fields to migrate as well as other animals such as bees, birds, and fish.[14] All living species rely on the earth's magnetic field. Ideally, we are also guided by this natural energy force. But unfortunately, this is not the case. Our compasses are constantly being pulled off course.

As depicted above, the earth's magnetic field has long lines between the northern and southern hemispheres, thus creating a natural magnetic field.[15] When we are in alignment with this natural magnetic field—for instance, being near bodies of water (oceans, lakes and rivers), plants, and trees—we experience increased overall health and well-being. When we are grounded to nature, we normalize our internal pH, reduce pain and inflammation, oxygenate the body, calm the brain, and experience better sleep, deeper rest, and relaxation.[16] Conversely, when we are around televisions, computers, cell phones, power lines, microwave ovens, radios, and cell towers, we are in a manufactured magnetic field consisting of short-range lines. These fields distort and throw us out of alignment with the long-range magnetic lines of the earth, creating dizziness, dis-ease, and disease. These short-range lines produce acid in our bodies, increase pain and inflammation, cause oxygen deficiency, disturb the brain's natural state, and lead to exhaustion.

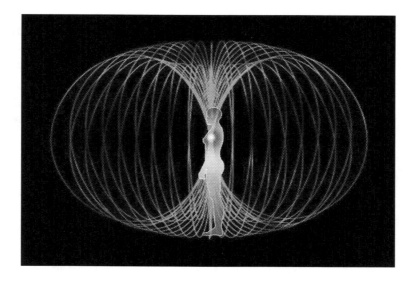

Today we sit indoors in front of various screens with the soles of our feet too often covered with synthetic materials, blocking us from receiving the healthy magnetic frequencies from the soul of the Earth. As a result, we are disconnected and drained. We are depleting our life-force, and we feel it.[17] Look at the above picture and notice how the field of energy rises from the earth up through the soles of the feet into the heart and out through the crown of the head. We can regenerate ourselves.

Many of us make sure our phones are charged, but what about us? Are we recharging our internal batteries?

Return to the source.

The earth relies on magnetic energy.

The human being relies on magnetic energy.

So, *why not our pedagogy?*

Magnetic Pedagogy

The heart of healing is love, and love is a magnet. The magnet never loses power. It's a force—just like love. When we are lost in ourselves and the world, the magnet can bring us back into purpose, to align us. How can teaching do this?

Energy exists within each of us, even if it may lay dormant. When we're aligned, we too become a force, like a magnet. When multiple magnets are aligned, our power increases. While this is metaphysical, it's also very practical.

Like all spiritual practices, magnetic pedagogy is an experience. It is a collective embodiment of energy. Perhaps you've felt this magnetism at a concert or other large gathering. It's that ubuntu energy—a connectivity that binds us together.

Unfortunately, we often don't think of our classrooms from this paradigm. But if you've ever been inside a magnetized classroom of inquiry, self-discovery, and community building, then you likely get this sensibility. The point here is not to make a manual on magnetic pedagogy but to rather uproot the technical mandates of schooling and consciously nurture new kinds of spaces where learning is alive and thrives.

Magnetic pedagogy is visceral, physical, and spiritual. Consider that pedagogy is the art, science, and soul of transformative learning. How then do we operationalize a soulful magnetism in the ways we teach? The answer is in the energy of being and becoming: supporting each student to tap into their own power for authenticity to thrive. This is easier said than done, and in the next chapter, we will delve into teaching toward sovereignty. For now, rest easy in the heart of the work and the sacred love we have for this legacy. The sacred transference between the teacher and student—like Hazrat Inayat Khan who taught Murshid Sam, who then initiated Farid Watson (Vajra's dad).

How is energy developed and shared inside classroom spaces? What are the sparks and how do they ignite other forms of curiosity? If energy is neither created nor destroyed, how then do we harmonize students toward one another?

Energy expands when each of us becomes an instrument in the collective choir of liberation. This means we've got to attune ourselves to the Uni-*verse*. Audre Lorde (1984) was right when she taught us to care for ourselves as an act of resistance. If we are not singing the alignment of our soul, we will be out of rhythm with the earth. Those around us can feel it! Positivity is real; it's a vibration that empowers and elevates. Inversely, negativity demeans and suffocates.

> *If you look at the people in your circle and don't get inspired,*
> *then you don't have a circle.*
> *You have a cage.*
> ~ Nipsey Hussle ~

When we teach toward the heart, learning is magnified, and our positive, collective energy expands. In *The Living Classroom*, Bache (2008) shares his years exploring "learning fields" that once activated, can turn basic lessons into great learning, "Learning that reaches into [students'] hearts as well as their minds, that lifts their vision to a new horizon and gives them insights they will draw on for years to come" (pp. 61–63).

Students feed off of the energy of the teacher who is mostly a facilitator. If the teacher is not a strong conductor of wisdom and self-discovery, curiosity often dwindles and dies. A magnetic pedagogy aligns students to their inner compass and purpose and builds on the energy of each person to generate learning. The classroom environment becomes alive and charged with humanizing and harmonizing electro-magnetic fields. There is a pulse to life, to ourselves, to our students, a vibration calling the soul to awaken.

Some essential lessons to consider:
- Pain is unavoidable but can serve as a tremendous teacher.
- As we heal, we strengthen our hearts and our capacity to love.
- Great learning is an undoing and a breaking open into something new, like the journey of the butterfly.
- Being in nature grounds and recharges the body, mind, heart, and soul.
- Magnetic pedagogy pulsates with positive energy and relies on individual authenticity as the basis for collective discovery.

Personal activity:
- Go outside. Find a piece of earth, uninterrupted with concrete, and sit or lie down.
- Imagine you are inside a cocoon. Slow down and let the earth love you. This is a practice in freedom.
- Write down how you feel afterwards. Are you recharged in any way?

Collective practice:
1. At first, have students recall and write about a painful event. Something they've experienced or witnessed, but instead of letting the story end, let it break open into imagination.
2. Inside this space of imagination, students rely on their creativity to finish the story. They now own the moment and control it, not the other way around.
3. How far can creativity take us into unlocking our natural powers?

As an example, check out this "re-telling" from Eve Ewing's (2017), *Electric Arches*. Notice the typed section is what actually occurred, and the hand-written verse is her creative power in-motion.

Into The Heart of Healing **89**

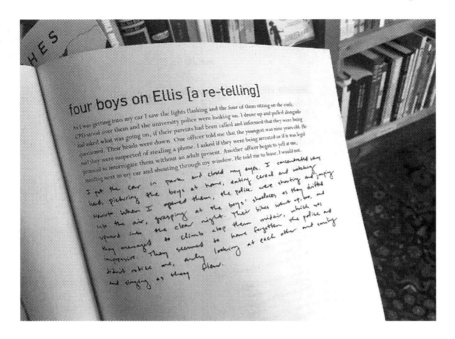

Got broken wings but I'm still fly
Baby, I'm tryna get closer, closer to GOD
~ D'Smoke ~

Notes

1. K. Gibran. (1980). *The Prophet*. New York: Alfred A. Knopf, pp. 52–53.
2. C. Barks, trans. (1995). *The Essential Rumi*. New York and San Francisco: Harper, p. 109.
3. Rebbe is another word for Rabbi.
4. P. Palmer. (2004). *A Hidden Wholeness*. San Francisco: Jossey-Bass, p. 181.
5. Photo from the movement of healing: www.themovementofhealing.com/?p=417. The text is from Peter Mayer *Heaven Below*. www.petermayer.net/music based on the *Kintsugi* tradition.
6. S. L. Lewis. (1981, 2012). *The Bowl of Saki Commentary*. San Francisco: Sufi Ruhaniat International, pp. 26–27.
7. C. Bourgeault. (2008). *The Wisdom Jesus*. Boston: Shambhala, p. 43.
8. The author of this spiritual story is unknown. Story taken from: www.Spiritual-Short-Stories.com.
9. E. Robert & Amidon, E. (1991). *Earth Prayers from Around the World: 365 Prayers, Poems and Invocations for Honoring the Earth*. New York: HarperCollins, p. 95.

10. Earth, Teach Me . . . Native American Quote, a poem by Chara, All Poetry.
11. P. Trimble. (1973). "Depatriarchalizing in Biblical Interpretation." *Journal of the American Academy of Religion*, 41 (1), 30–48. "Ambiguity characterizes the meaning of 'adham in Genesis 2–3. On the one hand, man is the first creature formed (2:7). The Lord God puts him in the garden "to till it and keep it," a job identified with the male (cf. 3:17–19). On the other hand, 'adham is a generic term for humankind. In commanding 'adham not to eat of the tree of knowledge of good and evil, the Deity is speaking to both the man and the woman (2:16–17). Until the differentiation of female and male (2:21–23), 'adham Is Basically Androgynous: One Creature Incorporating Two Sexes." eve_and_adam-text_analysis-2.pdf (csuohio.edu). See also P. Trimble. (1986). *God and the Rhetoric of Sexuality*. Minneapolis, MN: Fortress Press.
12. HeartMath institute. www.HeartMath.org.
13. P. Guerra, Gegear, R. & Reppert, S. (2014).
14. No compass needed: Honey bees are sensitive to Earth's magnetic polarity | (vassar.edu); Birds Can 'Read' The Earth's Magnetic Field To Find Their Way (forbes.com); Salmon Migrate Using Earth's Magnetic Field (nature.org).
15. Image from: https://theconversation.com/new-evidence-for-a-human-magnetic-sense-that-lets-your-brain-detect-the-earths-magnetic-field-113536.
16. See the D. Henry. (2014). "Stunning Health Effects of Magnetic Fields on Our Physiology." *Natural News*, June 29. www.naturalnews.com. See also C. Ober, Sinatra, S. T., Zucker, M., et al. (2010). *Earthing the Most Important Health Discovery Ever*. Laguna Beach, CA: Basic Health Publications; G. Chevalier, Sinatra, S. T., Oschman, J. L., Sokal, K. & Sokal, P. (2012). "Earthing: Health Implications of Reconnecting the Human Body to the Earth's Surface Electrons." *Journal of Environmental and Public Health*. https://doi.org/10.1155/2012/291541.
17. Source: www.in-light-ment.com.

8
TEACHING TOWARD SOVEREIGNTY

> *Got broken wings but I'm still fly*
> *Baby, I'm tryna get closer, closer to GOD*
> ~ D'Smoke ~

We purposely closed Chapter 7 and opened Chapter 8 with D'Smoke's call to get closer and closer to GOD. Think of sovereignty as the mountain, and we are the climb. The inner chamber of the heart has brought us to the soul, the core of our being, in which the inner light, the essence of who we are, radiates and permeates with magnetic might. Love is a magnet. And once aligned, we become a positive force of radical acceptance.

This power source is not gained through degrees or salaries, grants or tenure. It cannot be bought or sold. It is freely given, but it takes work. The intentional path of reconnecting ourselves to our Self—the essence of all life. It is this force which makes the sun shine, the birds sing, and the flowers blossom.

> *Don't gain the world and lose your soul;*
> *wisdom is better than silver or gold.*
> ~ Bob Marley ~

The soul of learning brings us even deeper inward to ask: Why am I here? How shall I live? In essence, *What is the pedagogy of my life?* We ask this because we cannot improve professionally until we transform personally. Who we are impacts how and what we teach. When there is no clarity around these answers, we are like a tree losing connection to its roots and, as a result, can be easily swayed by the opinion of others. To be sovereign in your inner-most being is to know your

DOI: 10.4324/9781003197164-8

roots and to connect to the life force that flows through them and nourishes them.

> *When the root is deep,*
> *there is no need to fear the wind.*
> ~ African Proverb ~

Let's consider some of the greatest teachers of sovereignty: Buddha, Jesus, and Muhammad. Buddha walked into the forest on a quest to find the remedy for suffering. Jesus went into the desert for 40 days to fast and pray. Muhammad went into a cave in Mount Hira. Each of them went into nature. Each of them fasted. Each of them went into the silence of themselves to listen to their soul and hear the voice of the Almighty. All being and becoming. The Alpha and Omega.

These prophets became vessels of alignment between heaven and earth, transient beings dancing to the sacred rhythm of the inner and outer worlds. Synchronizing the self in service. A sacred psalm. A balm in Gilead.

Oneness connects all life. And if all life is connected to and through GOD, then wherever we dwell, so does GOD dwell, too. While this is true, it's complicated. Finding enlightenment in the forest is one thing, but staying illuminated in the city is another.

What does this mean? The world did not drain or dissolve these awakened ones of their spiritual power. Even in the pains of exile and torture, their deep sense of purpose and faith was unflinching. These teachers became magnified through it! Love became the compass, vision, revelation, and direction.

What happened during these meditations that shapeshifted and reoriented these people's lives?

The transformation of Siddhartha into Buddha in the 6th century (B.C.E.) provides insight. Consider that even Buddha, in all his enlightenment, was enticed to stay in the forest, under the beautiful Bodhi tree. In Eknath Easwaran's (2007b) introduction to *The Dhammapada*, we learn the following:

> Mara, the tempter, appeared to Buddha once again and said, "You have awakened to nirvana and thus escaped from my realm. You have plumbed the depths of consciousness and known a joy not given even to the gods. But you know well how difficult it has been. You sought nirvana with your eyes clear, and found it almost impossible to achieve, other's eyes are covered with dust from the beginning and they seek only their own satisfaction. Even in the midst of sorrow, do you see anyone throw the toys of the world away? If you try to teach them what you have found, who do you think will listen? Who will strive as you have? How many will even try to wipe the dust from their eyes?"

For a long time, Buddha sat in silence, contemplating the impossibility of his mission. These questions shook him to the depths. In a world of sleepwalkers, how many would listen to someone returning from a world they would probably never see, coming to say that love always begets love and violence only breeds more violence? In a world guided by passions, who would be willing to make the sacrifices required to base their lives on these truths?

Slowly his confidence returned, "Perhaps" he replied, "there will be a few who will listen. Dust does cover the eyes of all. But for some it is only a thin film. Everyone desires an end to suffering and sorrow. To those who will listen, I will teach the dharma, and for those who follow it, the dharma itself will set them free" (pp. 40–41).

Buddha could have stayed under the tree! But instead, he left the forest because a few might listen to his lessons and embody them. This realization compelled him to connect with the world and serve as its teacher. The truth of his discovery lives on, amplifying, multiplying, and magnifying across generations.

Today there are over 535 million practicing Buddhists.

As this chapter illustrates, developing an inner compass is not for yourself alone; it can also be used in service to humanity. But it takes practice to develop your core such that your walk is your way. To put it in different words, traversing between the inner soul and the soul of the world takes an incredible amount of alignment and balance. To support the magnitude of this part of the journey, here are four essential steppingstones to help us reach the pinnacle of pedagogical possibilities:

1. To be sovereign is to know the Self.
2. The one who knows Self can become a sovereign teacher.
3. In turn, the sovereign teacher can support the sovereignty of each student.
4. The living classroom is magnetic.

My thing is that I don't give no person that much power over my path that I am walking. Not one person can make or break what I'm doing, except me or God.
~ Nipsey Hussle ~

To be sovereign is to know the Self.

There is a story called *The Question* about the great Hasidic master Rabbi Zusya. When Rabbi Zusya grew old and knew that his time on earth was nearing a close, his students were called around him. Timidly, one of them spoke and asked Rabbi Zusya what he was most afraid of about dying.

"I am most afraid of what they will ask me when I get to heaven," he answered.
"What will they ask you?" the disciples were eager to know.
"They will not ask me, 'Zusya, why were you not like Moses?'" he answered.
"They will ask me, 'Zusya, why were you not Zusya?'"[1]

We are all called to remember the truth of who we are. It is a remembering process, a reconnecting to our highest Self. Turn within first and plug into your internal power. These electro-magnetic waves are the pulse of life. When we're unable to live authentically, our electro-magnetic currents get stifled and disconnected and so does our teaching.

According to the *Vedas*, the True Self, *Atman* or heart-essence, is *sat-chit-ananda* (truth-consciousness-bliss)—boundless, unchanging and eternal. This energy gives our body, mind, heart and soul sentience. It can also magnify our teaching. Yet the ego, left undeveloped, distracts us from our inner magnificence and, as Acharya (2020) states, "we start believing the misconceptions" (p. 25). It is like saying, I am the bulb and forgetting the light. It is like the great river saying, I am the glass of water. We get attached to the world and forget the essence of our being.

The greatest knowing is to know oneself. In Egypt, this same maximum was inscribed onto the walls of the Temple of Luxor. In ancient Greece *Gnothi seauton* (Know thyself) was etched into the entrance of the Temple of Delphi.[2] This quest to know Self is also found within the Sanatana Dharma of India and, in Christianity and Islam. The *Upanishads* teach "The Self is Brahman"; "You are That" (*Chandogya Upanishad*). Jesus taught, "You who knows everything else but who does not know yourself knows nothing" (*The Gospel of Thomas*) and similarly, *The Hadith* states, "He who knows himself knows God" (Islam).

In our search for truth, we have come face-to-face with a painful reality. Most of us do not really know who or why we are. We may have had glimpses, but in actuality, it is a constant struggle to live deeply connected to the source of our being. When disconnected from ourselves, we are disconnected from our inner compass. *That perfect job becomes my north star.* We can get stuck seeking praise, power and prominence through external validations: allegiances to corporations, academic institutions, political associations or perhaps even religious organizations. That's the ego flexing its muscle and misdirecting our attention. Although we need substance to live, our allegiance to possessions will dispossess us.

What good will it be for someone to gain the whole world, yet forfeit their soul?
~ Matthew 16:26 ~

The journey to sovereignty is an ongoing search requiring guidance and practice. Along the way, we experience a deeper, truer Self that enlivens us from within. Even now, if you bring your attention to your hands, you can feel the pulsating life-force flowing through them. Do you feel the vibes? It's visceral and all-encompassing. Like a fish in water, we're living in fields of energies. Yet, we need to discern the energy fields we are living in. Is it healthy or unhealthy; healing or toxic? When the ego surrenders to the Self, *who* we really are can be found, nourished, and thrive. Living becomes more meaningful.

Even though we might want to quickly reach a destination of sovereignty, annihilate the ego, and prosper, please have mercy on yourself. Let's learn from the tree, like the Sequoia that lives for 3,000 years. The ripening tree does not force itself into bloom but surrenders to the seasons. It's a living manifestation of persistence and patience. Allow yourself to sink into your roots, the wisdom of your ancestors, and bloom seven generations forward. You are your living legacy.

Prayer for Sacred Pauses

Goddess of the sacred pause
please grant me the courage
to lay aside swiftness
and take up slowness,
to embrace limitations as learning,
silence as stabilizing,
waiting as worthy,
and sitting as divine.
Goddess of the sacred pause
help me to know stillness as strength,
patience as powerful,
and healing time
as holy necessity.
~ Molly Remer ~[3]

To transform the world, we have to actively commit to the transformation of ourselves and society. This is a daily commitment. A practice of seeing ourselves in relation to the world—not just recipients but the architects of it. Through this paradigm shift, we gain perspective and purpose. We do not accept all that we see as some form of manifest destiny. We look anew through eyes that are windows to the soul. This type of soul-work brings the inner journey outwards into the living, breathing, beautiful struggle of metamorphosis in the world. We become more discerning and yearn for the unification of compassion, courage, and care.

The compass becomes clearer: the quest to live free.
What is the Truth of this truth? _____

_____

What is your freedom dream? _____

_____
_____
_____

The one who knows Self can become a sovereign teacher.

In *The Courage to Teach* (1998), Palmer reminds us,

> Teaching, like any truly human activity, emerges from one's inwardness, for better or worse. As I teach, I project the condition of my soul onto my students, my subject, and our way of being together. The entanglements I experience in the classroom are often no more than the convolutions of my inner life. Viewed from this angle, teaching holds a mirror to the soul. If I am willing to look in that mirror and not run from what I see, I have a chance to gain self-knowledge and knowing myself is as crucial to good teaching as knowing my students and my subject (pp. 2–3).

A truly sovereign teacher is free and teaches from this state of freedom. A sovereign teacher is a revolutionary who has turned within. The central point being the soul and knowledge of self.

Karega Bailey (2019), a teacher in Oakland, California, is a supreme example of someone who looks into the mirror of the soul to find sovereignty. As a social-emotional healing practitioner and award-winning educator, he shares, "I acknowledge that there is a lot of pain in this world, but I am called to be in this world and not of it. The peace and joy I've been afforded has been paid for by Love" (p. 56). He continues,

> There is not enough darkness in the world
> to put out the light of even one candle,
> so never be afraid to let your light shine.
> And when you feel like life's hardships
> are dimming your light, it just may be an
> invitation into a new dimension of your inner light.
> ~ Karega Bailey ~[4]

Teaching is akin to candle lighting, the journey of illuminating hearts. However, each person can only light their own spark. So, the greatest teachers, then, are the ones who help students find their own light. In Ethiopia, there's a saying that *your parents give birth to you, but your teachers illuminate you.*

On Teaching

Then said a teacher, Speak to us of Teaching.

And he said:

No man can reveal to you aught but that
which already lies half asleep in the
dawning of your knowledge.

> The teacher who walks in the shadow of
> the temple, among his followers, gives not
> of his wisdom but rather of his faith and
> his lovingness.
>
> If he is indeed wise he does not bid you
> enter the house of his wisdom,
> but rather leads you to the threshold
> of your own mind.
>
> The astronomer may speak to you of his
> understanding of space,
> but he cannot give you his understanding.
>
> The musician may sing to you of the
> rhythm which is in all space,
> but he cannot give you the ear
> which arrests the rhythm nor the voice that echoes it.
>
> And he who is versed in the science of
> numbers can tell of the regions
> of weight and measure,
> but he cannot conduct you thither.
>
> For the vision of one man lends not its
> wings to another man.
>
> And even as each one of you stands alone
> in God's knowledge, so must each one of
> you be alone in his knowledge of God and
> in his understanding of the earth.
> ~ Kahlil Gibran ~[5]

The higher aspects of education reveal ourselves to ourselves. It's a living experience, not a subject matter. When we as teachers practice our humanity, learning becomes charismatic.

> *Face to face with my students, only one resource is at my immediate command:*
> *my identity, my selfhood, my sense of this "I" who teaches —*
> *without which I have no sense of the "Thou" who learns.*
> ~ Parker Palmer ~

What inspires and energizes you? _____
_____
_____

What inspires and energizes your students? _____
_____
_____

The sovereign teacher can support the sovereignty of each student.

Imagine a candle lighting another candle. Did the original candle lose its flame? No. Light expands light. Light magnifies with other lights. Let's get brighter in our beauty and brilliance! A magnetic pedagogy that supports and uplifts the sovereignty of the soul is glorious and contagious. So, what lessons take this theory and move it into practice? How do we ritualize self-discovery as a route toward sovereignty?

We know that *Who* we are is central to our teaching. And we know that *Who* our students are is essential to learning. Do we know our student's names? This is a simple question, with serious ramifications. Names help identify us amid and among our cultures, ancestors, place, and land. Naming is a process of locating us in space and time.

Similar to sacred teachings that refine our internal compass, names also play this essential function. Names help point us to ourselves. This is why the famous rapper Kendrick Lamar explains, "If I'm gonna tell a real story, I'm gonna start with my name." Let's be real with one another. Let's pronounce our names correctly.

In many places throughout the world, naming is not neutral; it is ceremonial. Names can serve as a compass of connection and self-determination. Sometimes people even feel the need to change or gather a new name to reflect a deeper truth of who they are and hope to become. This is because names have power: a conduit to our past and a path to our future, directly influencing our direction and pulling us toward some people and away from others. "I experience the Dharma as ancestral," explains Devin Berry. "It's all my ancestors sitting here—what they went through, what they survived, so that I could thrive."[6] Building on this idea, we can only be sovereign if we are first grounded and centered in the Self.

What is your name?
_____

What does your name mean?
_____

What names sound like home for you?
_____

To root us to reality, let's step toward our names. Here is an example from Linda Christensen (2015, p. 16) in *Rhythm and Resistance: Teaching Poetry for Social Justice*.

Linda Mae

My name sounds like a country-western singer
    wrangling cows and cowboy hearts
        out on the range.

    Linda Mae is my intimate name,
the name my family calls me when we're laughing,
    when there's blackberry pie on the table,
      and we spent the day swimming
    at Grizzly Creek or Swimmer's Delight.

My name is full of pinochle on summer nights,
      lit by stars and firelight.
    My name sounds like the jukebox
      at the Vista Del Mar
    where Dad poured Jack Daniels
        for fishermen
    while Mom served clam burgers
      And chicken fried steak.

    Linda Mae is the lonely child
    I became when my father died,
        the Linda
who crawled beneath the overturned skiff
        in the backyard,
    and lit candles in the dark curve
        of death.

    Linda Mae is the name
    Bill calls me when we're happy,
    when we hike Tamanawas Falls
      or watch salmon leap,
        silver acrobats
      climbing the white water
of the narrow Klickitat canyons.

    Linda Mae sounds like home.

Inspired by Linda's poem, write down three questions in which your full name is the answer to each question.

    Sample: "Whose mom would sing angels into the room when she was two years old? *Vajra Mujiba Watson.*"

Question 1: _____
Write your full name as the answer: _____

Question 2: _____
Write your full name as the answer: _____

Question 3: _____
Write your full name as the answer: _____

Poetry is the language of the soul. It can help students untie their tongues and traverse their feelings and ideas with meaning-making. Simple prompts like *what's your name* or *where I'm from* can open up the classroom space in profound ways (Watson, 2013, 2017). As each student gains sovereignty, there is personal and collective authenticity.

People are the authors of their own lives. Let their expertise shine.

The living classroom is magnetic

In the living classroom, everyone is a teacher, and everyone is a student. This is important. As alluded to in earlier chapters, in a traditional "banking concept" of schooling, students are the consumers of knowledge and information (see Freire, 1970). Whatever is deemed the "canon" is deposited into them, and they are required to regurgitate the facts in a particular manner and form. As Palmer finds, "The teacher-centered instructional model centers on a teacher who does little more than deliver prescribed conclusions to students" (pp. 118–119).

Subject + Teacher → Student outcomes

This equation provides a simple snapshot of the ways subjects are often taught in schools; they are mandated, decontextualized, and then evaluated. The process of redundancy rarely focuses on introspection and integrated learning. We are not teaching math, per se; rather, we are teaching living, breathing human beings, and our lessons should reflect this fact.

When students and teachers are viewed as active, valuable co-collaborators, then learning becomes a generative process of interaction and communion. The particular knowledge base on a subject matter (canon) becomes a dialogue partner in the learning process. In this milieu, learning serves as a synthesizing trifecta of text, teacher, and student. We get to know one another, build with one another, question and feed off each other's cultures and curiosities. It's experiential, exponential, and explosive. The classroom is alive!

This form of pedagogy has hands-on applications. Let's take a specific example to put this theory into practice. Vajra applied this pedagogy to the teaching of Nathaniel Hawthorn's *Scarlet Letter* (a district-wide mandated text written in 1850). For students at Grant Union High School in Sacramento, California, this was not a book they were particularly excited about or found relevant to their daily lives. Nevertheless, we proceeded.

Before *The Scarlet Letter* was ever introduced, the students were asked to write about revenge, which is a central theme of the story. It's important to reiterate this point: students examined revenge prior to ever seeing or being introduced to *The Scarlet Letter*. The students analyzed the concept of revenge from multiple vantage points through a variety of writing workshops that developed the student's multidimensional analysis of revenge. For instance, as depicted in the next figure, writing sprints and activities focused on moments they experienced revenge personally (self); examples of revenge at school and home (community); historical cases of revenge (past); and contemporary, political instances of revenge inter/nationally (present). When everyone had something to say—and their notebooks were full with free-writes, antidotes, and thesis statements about revenge—it was then that *The Scarlet Letter* was introduced to the class. When Hawthorne finally came into play, so to speak, the students were already experts on the deleterious and destructive nature of revenge and could enter into a dialectical and dialogical relationship with Hawthorne and each other.

Here is the shift in power: in a living classroom, students' lives and perspectives serve as the primary text from which they interact with the curriculum, not the other way around. Here is a visual representation of this process:

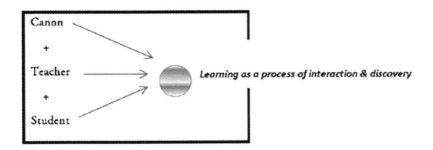

Any text, subject, or universal theme can serve as impetus for discovery that starts with knowledge of self. Consider a pebble: when it's thrown into a pond, there's a ripple effect. Now imagine the essential idea as the pebble: the pond is the student's lived experience and understanding of the world. Starting with the self allows the student to have an immediate response and expertise with the topic. From there, we go outward into family, community, history, present-day reality, and even into the future.

102 Teaching Toward Sovereignty

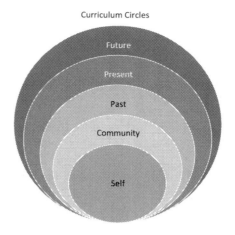

Curriculum Circles

In another example of student-centered instruction, Mary demonstrates how to embody learning. If knowledge is not embodied, does it have meaning? Aware of this essential question, Mary had her students bring their yoga mats to her composition course titled *Writing about Yoga*. To write about yoga, she teaches them the practice of yoga alongside reading and writing about it. In doing so, the students themselves became the living text and were better equipped to dialogue with other texts, both living and written. Students learned the asanas (poses) and practiced them. They also learned the Sanskrit terms and their meanings. As the semester progressed, students began to integrate their learning and were better able to express themselves in their writing, through a place of power and discernment. During the course, a student named Luke shared his experience:

> I began the semester with a lazy attitude. I simply wanted to hang out and basically do nothing. I was lethargic and apathetic . . . I just did not care, especially about schoolwork . . . I decided to care. I began to go inside myself, access my inner power and use it for good because of the influence of Garuda, the eagle. . . . Not only did I read the story, but each time we met in "Yoga and Writing" we would perform this pose (garudasana). Slowly, something started to seep into me, and I began to embody the lessons of Garuda. I too had felt small. I felt disempowered and disconnected from my potential. . . . The story taught me that although our size makes us feel small, we have endless power inside us.[7]

Luke went on to run for student government and win a seat for his class. While this was wonderful to witness, it was merely a manifestation of something deeper. Luke discovered his own inner light and became enlivened.

Bache (2004), in his article titled "High Octane Learning," explains that learning can become a symphony of souls:

> Everyone knows that words not supported by the energy of a person's experience carry much less power to influence others than words which are. This happens, I think, not because the words themselves are different or are delivered with a different inflection, but because when people speak, they unleash a tangible but invisible power into the space around them. The power comes ultimately from our experience and from the energetic access that our experience has created in us . . . In the playful dance of course content and energetic resonance, ordinary learning sometimes crosses a threshold to become Great Learning (pp. 35–36).[8]

We are magnificent beings, and when we connect to one another in sacred ways, our energy electrifies and crosses the threshold into "Great Learning."

The sovereign teacher is not trying to make students emulate someone else or become like them. S/he encourages them to make internal connections, creating balance between the students, the texts, and themselves—learning is introspective and interactive. The sovereign teacher actualizes discernment and positive discrimination (Carew and Lightfoot, 1979) to see each student as an individual filled with perspectives, possibilities, and answers.

Our uniqueness reveals our greatness.

> *When your soul is looking for you*
> *Light a candle on its path.*
> ~Rumi~

We long to hear the voice of the soul within us and join the soul voice among us. For this to occur, we've got to live and seek sovereignty. Be us truth-tellers, soul shakers, and movement makers.

> *The soul wants truth, not trivia.*
> *So, if the space between us*
> *is to welcome the soul,*
> *it must be a space in which truth can be told.*
> ~ Parker Palmer ~

When our sovereignty is aligned, we can make the climb. We begin to see and experience ourselves and our students with renewed capabilities. Not only do our students begin to change, but our students also change us. In totality, it's an act of collective transformation.

As we reach toward this summit, may we open our textbooks, our notebooks, and ourselves—alongside our students—with renewed sensibilities, courageous capabilities, and dare to do education differently. Applying these concepts to the classroom is relatively new, yet teaching demands something more if we are to decolonize and revolutionize the ways we learn. We need classrooms that are both analytical and emotional, scientific and spiritual, theoretical and practical.[9]

Combined with the art and science of teaching, a classroom with soul alters our pedagogical axis. We become something greater—a force of whole-making. Magnetic, attractive, generous, and powerful. Healthy, soulful magnetic pedagogy pulls and pushes, stretches and strengthens, and energizes and enlightens. It's both the journey and the destination of learning! Ah, learning is my love language! Love can help us transform ourselves and even farther outward into our schools, universities, and communities.

When the magnet of our heart turns into pure love, this enables us to unite, and in that unity, to yearn for and embody living justice.

―――

The essential lessons to consider:

- We are moving from the reading of lessons, into the doing of practices.
- Remember, you are the key to your own sovereignty.
- To practice your purpose, develop a personal activity that celebrates your unique gifts.
- As a creative practitioner, design a collective practice that joins people together to honor their individual differences.

Slow down and let me love you.
~ Skip Marley and H.E.R. ~

Notes

1. E. Davy Pearmain, ed. (2007). *Doorways to the Soul: 52 Wisdom Tales from Around the World*. Eugene, OR: Resource Publications, p. 123.
2. Translated as "Know Thyself." This phrase was one of three phrases inscribed at the Temple of Delphi. The other two were "nothing in excess" and "surety brings ruin."
3. M. Remer. (2019). "Prayer for Sacred Pauses." *Brigid's Grove*, June 15 (via Make Believe Boutique).
4. K. Bailey. (2019). *Sol Affirmations: A Tool Kit for Reflection and Manifesting the Light Within*. New York: Self-Published, p. 1.
5. K. Gibran. (1980). *The Prophet*. New York: Alfred A. Knopf, pp. 56–57.
6. Shared by: *Insight Meditation Society*.
7. M. Keator. (2019). "Writing About Yoga: Lectio Divina and the Awakening of the Soul." In *The Whole Person: Embodying Teaching and Learning Through Lectio and Visio Divina*. New York: Rowman & Littlefield, p. 62.
8. C. M. Bache. (2004–2005). "High Octane Learning." *Shift: At the Frontiers of Consciousness* (5), 35–36.
9. The visual depiction of the art, science, and soul of transformative learning is taken from V. Watson. (2017). "Life as Primary Text: English Classrooms as Sites for Soulful Learning." Invited submission for *The Journal of the Assembly for Expanded Perspectives on Learning*, 22, 16, an affiliate of the National Council of Teachers of English.

9
BELOVED COMMUNITY

*Our goal is to create a beloved community and
this will require a qualitative change in our souls
as well as a quantitative change in our lives.*
~ Reverend Dr. Martin Luther King, Jr. ~

The Soul of Learning is spiritually grounding and pedagogically centering, yet our quest for a better world is never-ending. Inequality is grueling and gruesome. It might be easier to turn away—to cocoon. While this kind of isolation is necessary and can be revelatory, even Moses had to come down from the mountain and back into the wonders and woes of the world.

*Moses was there with the Lord forty days and forty nights
without eating bread or drinking water.
He wrote on the tablets the words of the covenant—the Ten Commandments.
And when Moses came down from Mount Sinai
with the two tablets of the Testimony in his hands,
he was unaware that his face had become radiant from speaking with the Lord.*
~ Exodus 34:28–29 ~

There are so many similarities among the world's religions. Moses fasted, turned inward, and heard the voice of the Most High. Some scholars of the Old Testament believe the scripture describes him being in the presence of "myriads of holy angels."[1] The fasting, prayer, and revelation of Moses are no different than those of Buddha, Jesus, or Muhammad. For all of our divisions, there is a oneness here.

DOI: 10.4324/9781003197164-9

These beautiful guides demonstrate the walk of enlightenment. What was revealed to them in their solitude, they shared in service with humanity. Although higher and deeper wisdom had awakened within them, they did not use it to rule over others. As the activist is called to go in and contemplate, the contemplative is called to go out into the world and activate. And although the earth is majestic and glorious, the world is filled with heart-aching, soul-wrenching oppression. It is all around us, but it ain't pretty. We must open our eyes and never be complacent or complicit. When we discover the balance between the inner and outer world, we go from seeking justice to living justice.

> *Raise the standard*
> *by which you judge*
> *yourself—and by which*
> *you are willing to be judged.*
> ~ H.I.M. Haile Selassie I ~

Awakening is a gift that comes with responsibility. Reciprocity and respect. Descending down the mountain, we come face-to-face with a time and a place.

Today is April 21, 2021

It has been over a year since the world went into lock down over COVID-19. And still there is no resolve. Many people have lost jobs with no recourse, unable to collect unemployment, no sense of where the funds will come to pay their bills, clothe their children, feed their families. People are scared, people are suffering, and people are dying.

> *We can disagree and still love each other unless your disagreement*
> *is rooted in my oppression and denial of my humanity and right to exist.*
> ~ James Baldwin ~

In this very moment, women and children are being molested, raped, and trafficked across borders and locked in cages. Murders are occurring in the streets. We are so far away from beloved community. The turmoil of our divisions is visceral.

Yesterday, in a historic moment, Minnesota police officer Derek Chauvin was held accountable for the murder of George Floyd. Reprieve. As people cried out in jubilation for this conviction, at the exact same time, a police officer in Columbus, Ohio, was killing 16-year-old Ma'Khia Bryant. If police can arrest white people who are mass shooters carrying assault rifles, then why were they unable to peacefully detain a young Black girl? Ma'Khia called 9–1–1 for help and protection, the police arrived on the scene, and they murdered her. Following her death, the police shouted to onlookers, "Blue Lives Matter!"[2]

Days before, Minnesota police officers killed Daunte Wright, a 20-year-old young Black man during a routine traffic stop. The next day, camera footage was released showing the murder of Adam Toledo, a 13-year-old seventh grade Latino student in Chicago, Illinois. He, too, was killed by law enforcement officers. All of this in a week. And this is just the headlines based on body cameras and street footage.

All around the world, we see people gathered in the streets taking back their power. No longer dependent on mainstream news, social media allows us to share on the ground, in-time information. White people, in particular, are now able to see—in living color—the police brutality aimed at Black people. Many of us have watched, in disbelief, the recurring videos.

Home-made cell phone videos that go viral; hashtags that invoke protests. In fact, technology has brought us closer to each other than ever before; we can literally see into each other's eyes. Social media, for all of its negative effects—and there are many—has also reconfigured our connections and collective calling. We cannot turn away from the wailing. It is a meditation in mourning.

Today is also the Ninth day of Ramadan

Every year, Muslims around the world anticipate the sighting of the new crescent moon that signifies the official first day of Ramadan, the ninth month of the Islamic calendar, when the Holy Qur'an was dictated to Prophet Muhammad (*Sallallahu Alai-hi Wassallam*)[3] by the angel Gabriel. Since Muhammad could not read or write, he first dictated the Qur'an to his wife, Khadija, who was the first scribe and believer. To this day, she is considered the mother of Islam.

In this time of fasting, Muslims abstain from food and drink to contemplate and experience closer connections to the divine and develop compassion for the poor and hungry. Fasting forces us inward and helps us see ourselves and the world anew. Ramadan brings us into the horizon of our lives—a divine connection between sky and earth, between past ancestry and future possibility.

Ramadan is also considered the month of mercy, and Ramadan reflects the moon.[4] The moon and the sun live together in a sacred dance with the earth. Yin and Yang. We give witness and experience these cycles that are intricately connected. While the moon's beams cool, soothe, and nourish, the sun's rays warm, enliven, and energize. A harmonization of opposites.

Now consider that justice—literally and figuratively—requires balance. Visualize the *Scales of Justice*, which symbolize the needs of an individual on the one hand and the demands of society on the other. The symbol of truth and justice is ancient, dating back to Kemet (Egypt) and the Goddess of Justice, *Ma'at*. Ma'at helps turn chaos into creation and restores order to life—much like Lord Vishnu in Hinduism. In her hands, she holds the scales, measuring our heart against a feather.

To seek justice, find truth. Truth is like gravity; it pulls us back to reality.

Interconnections are profound, pulsating with life, and poetic:

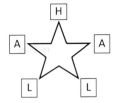

Building on a cosmology of divine order and unity, Five Percenters[5] reason that the Self is a microcosm of the universe. To represent this worldview in English, in the depiction shown above, *A*rm, *L*eg, *L*eg, *A*rm, *H*ead represents our body and spells out *ALLAH*.

We are in this world. We are not separate from *this* land, moon, or sun. GOD is out there and in here. We are one! But why then do we kill one another? If we're all related, then what's the purpose of tearing ourselves apart? More important, how do we put humanity back together?

In Lak'ech

Tú eres mi otro yo.
You are my other me.
Si te hago daño a ti,
If I do harm to you,
Me hago daño a mi mismo.
I do harm to myself.
Si te amo y respeto,
If I love and respect you,
Me amo y respeto yo.
I love and respect myself.
~ Luis Valdez ~[6]

A Healing

Alongside Ramadan, today is also the holy Groundation for Rastas around the world. A day of repatriation, retribution, and revelation. On April 21, 1966, King Haile Selassie I of Ethiopia traveled to Jamaica and, for many, fulfilled a prophetic need to reunite African people around the world. This visit built on Selassie's monumental decree in 1948 to provide 500 acres of land at Shashamene[7] to Black people from the Western Hemisphere—descendants of those who were stolen and enslaved—to find their way back home.

While the gift of land is historic and land is power, nobody should have to return to their place of ancestral origin for soil and sovereignty. A Black farmer in California once said, "Africa is anywhere I plant my feet and seeds." This kind of outlook abolishes borders while growing an even deeper connection to our roots.

> *The tried to bury us,*
> *they didn't know we were seeds.*
> ~ Mexican Proverb ~

Similar to plants, what we are able to grow is based, in large part, on the seeds buried within us.

Inside the beloved community, there is a commitment to heal. And address wrongdoings, like the *Truth and Reconciliation Commission* assembled in South Africa after the legal end of apartheid. It is reparations and repairing harm. The work is individual, interpersonal, and institutional. Cultural, historical, and political.

> we need a r/evolution of the mind.
> we need a r/evolution of the heart.
> we need a r/evolution of the spirit.
> the power of the people is stronger than any weapon.
> a people's r/evolution can't be stopped.
> we need to be weapons of mass construction.
> weapons of mass love.
> it's not enough just to change the system.
> we need to change ourselves.
> ~ Assata Sharkur ~

Tomorrow

April 22, 2021. It is spring. A time of renewal. Life is birthing, bursting, and blooming all around us. There are birds chirping outside, overcast skies, and massive social unrest. Prayer and protest. Joy and justice. Prophesy and poetry. So much might and beauty. Abolition of oppression is a reality, and it's possible. Let's get there—*together!*

People power. We are sovereign beings. Our dignity, worth, and freedom are not man-made or corporate given—these are falsehoods and fallacies. In beloved community, racism cannot exist. Human trafficking stops. Domination dies. This is why our internal work is so important. We turn within to dig up the insidious and inherited roots of oppression that have burrowed into our psyche. Looking within, we must ask ourselves, *How has my privilege diminished the privilege of others? How has my own personal evolution and increased integrity contributed to a more wholesome world?* It is hard work, a continuous flow—in and out—day in and day out. Like inhaling and exhaling, one moment at a time.

> *For hatred does not cease by hatred*
> *at any time:*
> *Hatred ceases by love.*
> *This is an unalterable law.*
> ~ Buddha ~

Domination is finite. Humanity's yearning for community is infinite. Love is an experience of the infinite. When woven together, the fruit of contemplation and social justice is raw, real, agape love. Not paternalistic, missionary love but love that transcends and connects people across generations, geographies, and genealogies. Love without contemplation can become naïve and self-serving,[8] whereas love without justice can remain ethereal, even hokey (Duncan-Andrade, 2009). We *must* integrate the two. This real-world quest for equity is the material manifestation of love on earth. hooks (2013) reflected on her encounters with activists. She was struck that "it was always love that created the motivation for profound inner and outer transformation." She contends, "Love was the force that empowered folks to resist domination and create new ways of living and being in the world" (p. 195). Echoing this same sentiment, Greg Boyle, founder of Homeboy Industries and author of *Tattoos on the Heart*, commonly shares, rather emphatically, that "there is no *them* and *us*. There is only *Us!*"

> *How long shall they kill our prophets*
> *While we stand aside and look? Ooh*
> *Some say it's just a part of it*
> *We've got to fulfill the book*
> *Won't you help to sing*
> *These songs of freedom?*
> *'Cause all I ever have*
> *Redemption songs*
> ~ Bob Marley ~

We are all intricately and delicately connected—body, mind, heart, soul; therefore, how we see and care for ourselves influence how we see and care for one another. Revolution is in the hard work of justice, but it is also found in the grace of gentleness and joy. Play can be revolutionary. It is honest, intimate, and spontaneous. A place where intuitive consciousness and imagination meet. It is present oriented and process oriented, not product driven. Through play, song, and practicing vulnerability, we open ourselves to envision, create, and manifest harmonious horizons.

Future

Today is: _____

What is happening today? _____
_____
_____
_____

How are you teaching toward the future you want? _____
_____
_____
_____

Teaching Love

Education is a journey toward reality, reckoning, reprioritizing, and reconnecting. Authentic love is the magnet that generates and holds this kind of learning energy together. What would we experience if we shared different seeds—those older origin stories that reach deeper into the common roots of our existence and resistance? Would we develop a healthier outlook on life itself? Able to grow more fully human in and through our differences?

> *A flower does not think of competing*
> *with the flower next to it.*
> *It just blooms.*
> ~ Zen Shin ~

Part of fostering beloved community is teaching through different eyes. This is not just counter-hegemonic; it is grounded to a worldview that predates borders, walls, and ownership. There was life before colonialism and vast civilizations prior to European imperialism (Browder, 1992; Clarke, 1993; Diop, 1974; Jackson, 1985; Rogers, 1972; Sertima, 1976, 1992).

> *The greatest teachers of humanity become streams of love.*
> ~ Hazrat Inayat Khan ~

Harmonious ways of being are diametrically opposed and incongruous to Western, colonial structures that rely on divisions, hierarchies, and inequalities. Let us consider that in *Education and the Aim of Human Life*, Pavitra (1961) discloses, "You must find, in the depths of your being, that which carries in it the seed of universality, limitless expansion, timeless continuity. Then you decentralize, spread out, enlarge yourself; you begin to live in everything and in all beings; the barriers separating individuals from each other break down" (p. 74). Building on this worldview, there is a similar word in South Africa—ubuntu—that reflects a profound idea that humanity is bound together in ways that are invisible to the eye yet gripping to the soul—a oneness that inspires compassion and ignites innovation. As Desmond Tutu states, "I am because you are. My humanity is inextricably bound up in yours." Rastas use the term "I-and-I" to denote the same idea of coexistence and harmony. I-and-I is used as a substitute for "me" and "you," which Rastas consider exclusionary, divisive words. Since there is divinity in all beings, I-and-I becomes the linguistic expression of this tradition.

Learning can heal and in doing so become an intersection to discover and reclaim sacred struggle.

> *And if you've ever been in love*
> *Then you'd understand*
> *~ Lauryn Hill ~*

If you've ever felt love or been in love, you've experienced the spark. An indescribable magnetic energy that pulls like a force of attraction. This drawing toward is not just sexual in nature. We can be drawn toward each other and life itself in thousands of different ways—both healthy and unhealthy. But a magnetic pedagogy that pulsates with the power of unconditional love is the magnet that can hold and pull and put humanity back together.

This kind of transformative teaching praxis does not just live in our heads but also in our hearts—and most definitely in our hands and feet. In other words, it is not merely what is conceived that is revolutionary but what is achieved, daily, in how we are *living justice*.

> *Although we are not one, we are not separate.*
> *And although we are not separate, we are not the same.*
> *~ Sebene Selassie ~*

Beloved community is not about sameness; it is about the unification of differences. This kind of togetherness is achieved through the magnetism of love. Beloved community *is* belonging. Belonging to ourselves and one another. Belonging to the fight for equity and the quest for truth. Belonging to the land, the universe, each and every day. It is vision and manifestation. And while this struggle to change the world is definitely real, it's also really beautiful and harmonious—like a better future calling us forward.

> *Our strategy should be not only to confront empire, but to lay siege to it.*
> *To deprive it of oxygen. To shame it.*
> *To mock it with our art, our music, our literature, our stubbornness, our joy,*
> *our brilliance, our sheer relentlessness—and our ability to tell our own stories. . .*
> *On a quiet day, I can hear her breathing.*
> *~ Arundhati Roy ~*

Similar to Arundhati Roy, we can also hear her breathing.

―――

Nature serves as an extraordinary role model that differences and opposites can co-exist. But to actualize harmony with one another can be extremely challenging. *Am I attached to my ideas, thoughts, or beliefs?* Beloved community moves us from hearing to listening. In this milieu, listening is an act and an ethic of care—a way to deeply learn from one another.

Collective Practice: Creating a Listening Café

In *The World Café*, Brown and Isaasc (2005), share that "we humans want to talk about things that matter to us. In fact, this is what gives satisfaction and meaning to life. Second, as we talk together, we are able to access a greater wisdom that is found only in the collective" (p. ix). However, to access this greater wisdom, we first need to learn how to listen, not through our own preconceived perceptions, notions and emotions but through an authentic willingness to bend our ear toward the heart of another. "It is through this process of attentive listening, dialogue and communal sharing of life experiences that new insights arise" (Keator, 2020b). To listen this way takes trustful practice.

To create a listening café, gather students into small groups. Next select terms from the list, placing one in the center of each table or /group. Taking turns (within a timed-session, one to two minutes), students reflect and share what this word means to them, while the others in the group listen attentively. There is no debate, and there is no dialogue. Participants in the group give the speaker their undivided attention. After time is up, students scatter to different tables, with a different word, and begin the process again. Since students do not always sit with the same groupings, they will have an opportunity to listen to various perspectives throughout the listening sessions. The listening activity can also be conducted with quotes, questions, poems, and stories throughout the book. At the end of the activity, students can share what they heard and learned.

ESSENTIAL WORDS TO CONSIDER AND DEFINE

Abolition:
_____

Abundance:
_____

Activist:
_____

Agency:
_____

Authenticity:
_____

Awakening:
_____

Community:
_____

Consciousness:
_____

Contemplative:

Cooperation:

Courage:

Create:

Education:

Expert:

Freedom:

Future:

Gratitude:

Harmony:

Heart:

Healing:

Human:

Humility:

Joy:

Learning:

Liberation:

Listening:

Living justice:

Love:

Magnetic pedagogy:

Meditation:

Mind:

Past:

Peace:

Power:

Present:

Purpose:

Resistance:

Revolution:

Rituals of awakening:

School:

Self:

Soul:

Soul of learning:

Sovereignty:

Spiritual:

Truth:

Unity:

Wisdom:

Contemplate this essence: *How are you learning and living these words?*

Notes

1. J. P. Schultz. (1971). "Angelic Opposition to the Ascension of Moses and the Revelation of the Law." *The Jewish Quarterly Review*, 61 (4), 282–307.
2. For further information on this case, visit www.essence.com/news/makiyah-bryant-fatally-shot-by-blue-lives-matter-police.
3. Peace and blessings be upon him.
4. While the Western Gregorian calendar is based on the sun, the Islamic calendar follows a lunar tradition.
5. The Five-Percent Nation, sometimes referred to as the Nation of Gods and Earths (NGE/NOGE), was founded in 1964 in Harlem, New York.
6. In Mayan culture, the law of *In Lak'ech Ala K'in* means "I am you, and you are me." Chicano playwright Luis Valdez adopted this concept and put it into a poem. An excerpt from this poem was recited by students in Arizona schools until it was outlawed by the state legislature in 2010 for "politicizing students and breeding resentment against whites."
7. Shashamane is located in the Oromo region of Ethiopia, about 150 miles from the capital of Addis Ababa.
8. Thomas Merton, an activist and monk, shared, "He who attempts to act and do things for others or for the world without deepening in own self-understanding, freedom, integrity and capacity to love, will not have anything to give others. He will communicate to them nothing but the contagion of his own obsessions, his aggressiveness, his ego-centered ambitions, his delusions about ends and means, his doctrinaire prejudices and ideas. There is nothing more tragic in the modern world than the misuse of power and action." Cited in R. Rohr. (2016). "The Activist's Guide to Contemplation." *Sojourners*, May 23.

10
ANCIENT FUTURES

*If you want to go fast, go alone,
If you want to go far, go together.*
~ African Proverb ~

The Soul of Learning has been a journey, taking us through the portal of awareness, authenticity, and awakening. It's been slow and intense, filled with introspection and insight. We've been traveling through this work together. We made a conscious choice to walks these words side by side (as co-authors) and make an earnest attempt to connect disparate traditions and disciplines. In all honesty, if we'd written by ourselves or just wrote solo chapters, it would have been easier and faster. But the world yearns for communion, so we had to honor the process. There are times when Mary's voice is more prominent or Vajra's style comes to the center, and that's okay. It's akin to the collaborative nature of geese.

Picture the geese migrating across the sky in a V formation. Have you seen it? The lead bird's role is not simply to guide the other birds but to reduce air drag so the flock can fly greater distance without expending more energy. Moreover, each bird in the flock takes a turn leading the formation. For the geese, there is no hierarchy. Rather, it's a matter of who has the ability in the moment to offer greatest support to get the group to the destination. This famous V formation is not static but constantly in motion because everyone is taking turns and taking a break. The flock evenly distributes the workload over the long journey. These beautiful birds cover 70% more distance than if they flew alone. They teach us about life and leadership.

Who is in your V formation? _____

___

DOI: 10.4324/9781003197164-10

So many of us live, work, and think in silos. Even teaching can feel incredibly isolating: "my classroom and my students." Although this might seem extreme, there are always areas in our lives that long for further belonging.

What stops you from being more collaborative? _____
_____
_____

What hinders you from developing deeper connections? _____
_____
_____
_____

As human beings, we are beautifully unique. And that's our superpower. Instead of our differences dividing us they can cultivate compassion, cooperation, and community. There is unity in diversity. As Sri Aurobindo shared, "We see that in this harmony between our unity and our diversity lies the secret of life; Nature insists equally in all her works upon unity and upon variation. We shall find that a real spiritual and psychological unity can allow a free diversity."[1]

When we engage in collaborative practices, we open up ourselves to others. This can feel intimidating and even downright terrifying. What if my thoughts and ideas are rejected? What if I am rejected? We must weigh the cost, the upside potential versus the downside risk. However, the truth is that some of the greatest concepts happen when people who hold different perspectives listen to one another. It is in hearing and working *with* each other that we are stretched to think and act in mightier ways.

Shawn Ginwright (2015) calls forth "healing justice," a way to understand the relationship between social justice and spirit work. His scholarship focuses on the consequences of systemic oppression and the hope and agency that exist to restore vibrant ways of living. Healing-centered teaching and community organizing recognizes that healing is political, healing and organizing intersect, and healing is found in culture, collaboration, and spirituality.

In and through diverse connections, our soul can expand, while our relationship to ourselves and the earth deepens. We gain glimpses into the lives of one another—the complications, idiosyncrasies, and commonalities. We're all going through something, and this Jewish tale brings this poignant lesson to life.

Tree of Sorrows

In a small village in Poland, there lived a wise rabbi. His followers loved him and came often to tell him of their woes. After a while, the rabbi grew tired of hearing each one claim that their lot in life was so much more difficult to bear than their neighbor's. They were constantly asking, "Why doesn't he have to suffer as I do? Why doesn't she have a nagging husband, or why doesn't he have a lazy wife? Why doesn't she have back trouble, and why don't his children still live at home, contributing nothing to the family's income?" On and on it went until the rabbi came up with a plan.

He sent out word that there was to be a new holiday celebrated. "Bring your sorrows and troubles," he announced. "Bring them in a bag with your name on it and hang the bag from the great tree in the center of the village. All will be allowed to exchange troubles and to go home with those of your neighbor rather than your own."

The villagers were excited, imagining how much easier their lives would be from that day on. When the day came, they assembled beneath the tree with bags in hand. With bits of rope, they tied their bags to the low branches of the tree so that all might inspect them. "Now," said the rabbi in a very official voice, "if you will all move about inspecting the bags, you may choose someone else's troubles to take home, thus freeing yourselves from your own."

The villagers rushed at the tree and began grabbing at and peering into bags, one after the other, around and around, around and around the tree. . . . Finally, quite tired out and feeling both foolish and wiser, they each sought out their own bags and walked home. The rabbi smiled. It was just as he had hoped. The villagers had seen the sorrows of others as they really were and had decided to stick with their own lots in life because, at least, they were familiar.[2]

Often, we can get preoccupied with comparing ourselves to others. Through this tale, we learn that we all carry the weight of the world in different ways. When the villagers looked into each other's woes, they came to appreciate their own lot in life. They also had more compassion for one another. When we engage in these types of exercises, others become more human in our eyes, while we too, become more humane. While some woes are definitely heavier than others, suffering is universal. Is there a way to not suffer alone, but heal together?

*When a person's level of consciousness raises,
lower tendencies such as hatred, greed, and anger
fall away from his nature like dry leaves and
higher attributes such as generosity and compassion,
grow in equal proportion.*
~ Shriram Sharma Acharya[3] ~

Are you the same being who first picked up this book? Has your perspective expanded, your heart softened, your soul brightened? Are you more awake and aware? Perhaps you feel a bit of inner spaciousness, calm, or clarity. If you consider carefully your journey through this portal, you are not the same; we are not the same. Together we took measured steps, participating in sacred practices that renew and replenish. We hope you were able to peer into the pages of this book alongside peering into the mirror of your own life. Maybe there are chapters in which you leaned in a little closer to listen to ancient wisdom, saw yourself reflected in a poem, or felt the way learning can breathe through you. Our intention was to create an embodied practice that was transformative, collaborative, and experiential.

We learn by doing, not just in knowing.

As our time together comes to a close, it's more than a call to arms. It's about longer arms reaching so far out and around the earth, creating an embrace of compassion and care. A righteous frequency of living justice that is rebellious and restorative because it is guided by revolutionary love. This is easier said than done, but once you experience it, it shapeshifts your understanding of what's possible. We are divinely, collaboratively capable of being and becoming soulful beings.

> *Pray through doing.*
> *Pray through digging*
> *and when we do it in community*
> *and when we do it together*
> *that's what ceremony is.*
> *~ Kyle Lemle ~*[4]

As a direct result of Vajra's long-standing work with United Playaz (UP),[5] a youth leadership and violence prevention organization in San Francisco, California, she was given the opportunity to partake in an event to turn "lead into life."[6]

Below is her journal excerpt:

> I'd been hearing from Rudy Corpuz, Jr. of United Playaz that we were going to take part in an event on MLK's birthday where we'd be bringing the weapons we collected from this year's annual gun buy-pack program and melting them down into shovels. While I was ready to participate, I didn't realize I would be partaking in a sacred ceremony. Here's what happened.
>
> I have on my United Playaz regalia. I arrive at Oscar Grant Plaza in Oakland, and I'm told that I'm going to be tossing one of the guns into the kiln. When the sun is high in the sky, I sit on the sidelines waiting. Throughout the afternoon, I listen to mothers cry out in pain because they buried their children too soon, and watch countless people collectively construct a large altar. It seems that everything happening is intentional, and also intuitive. And then as the sun begins to set, the drumming gets louder.
>
> Hundreds of people are out here! All ages. As the sky darkens, the ritual begins. Singers and dancers form a procession and encircle the handmade kiln created in real-time for this occasion. I am in the processional line now, experiencing the transcendence.
>
> *I choose a gun from the basket.*
> *I say a prayer.*
> *I hand it over into the fire.*
> *It burns.*

The flow of metal lava that pours out of the kiln takes the shape of a constellation. Yet, I only realize this because I am inside the circle. Someone turns to me and says, "You know that this is how the stars looked when Oscar Grant was murdered by the police? We built this to connect sky and earth, and to bring him here. He is with us." There is weeping and laughter simultaneously. Children sitting on top of shoulders clapping their hands in unison. Singing and poetry. It feels radical and heavenly.

As soon as I get home, I look up the visionaries who created this space and read, "Our intention through Lead to Life is to transform that which ends life into that which sustains life—to facilitate an alchemical healing process that can physically transform both our weapons and our imaginations." I can hear the Bible verse ringing in my ears: "They shall beat their swords into plowshares . . . nation shall not lift up sword against nation, neither shall they learn war anymore" (Isaiah 2:4).

Etched into each shovel are the following words:

As we decompose violence, may the Earth again be free.

Energy is neither created nor destroyed, but it can be transformed. It is about our intention, attention and determination. What are we willing to imagine and create anew? Both the gun and the shovel are made of the same metal; one was used for death, the other for life. Just as we work to harmonize our inner world, we, too, must work to harmonize our outer world. And just like we work to harmonize the outer world, we, too, must work to harmonize our inner world. It's a balance of vibrations.

> *The outer work can never be small*
> *If the inner work is great.*
> *And the outer work can never be great*
> *If the inner work is small.*
> ~ Meister Eckhart ~

Connecting the inner and outer worlds takes vision, action, and reflection. Turning again to the wisdom of bell hooks (2009), she teaches: "Our theory was far more progressive and inclusive in its vision than our everyday life practice. . . . Many of us found that it was easier to name the problem and deconstruct it, and yet it was hard to create theories that would help us build community, help us border cross with the intention of truly remaining connected in a space of difference long enough to be transformed" (p. 2). We land, yet again, on this notion of transformation that relates to a kind of metamorphosis. The humility and willingness to change and let go—to shed—*so we can fly*.

We can problematize everything; what does it mean to be a solutionary?

_____

_____

_____

_____

_____

> *The arc of the moral universe is long,*
> *but it bends toward justice.*
> ~ Reverend Dr. Martin Luther King, Jr. ~

Racial justice turns othering into belonging, igniting our collective possibilities. It's a way of becoming. Holistic and holy. Abolishing unjust borders while finding healthy boundaries. Being in the world but not completely of it. Maybe this is what it feels like to be human and have wings, going higher, flying farther - like the geese - to see bolder horizons.

While abolishing false ideas and ideals, we awaken to deeper and higher truths: messy truth, moving truth, magnificent truth. As we liberate ourselves, we liberate education. This leads us into beloved community which is predicated on trust. Trust can rebuild us, but it takes concerted effort and courageous action.

Being human is not a noun but a verb. Being human is a praxis of humanness.

The work before us does not end with who do I want to become; it also entails what legacy I want to grow forward. In *The Scholar as Human*, Peters (2021) discusses the "disembodied voice" that comes from divorcing ourselves from connection. He writes, "as human beings" we are "larger and more complicated than the positions" we occupy or roles we play. As we unfold into this "living, breathing reality" we partake in a kind of "prophetic aspiration" (pp. 248–264).

We are inside this portal of prophetic aspiration. A portal. Past made present. And present made future. Opening time. All of us giving birth and delivering realities beyond us. We are becoming into being.

We are the ancestors of tomorrow.

Who do you want to become? _____

_____

What kind of ancestor will you be? _____

_____

Now let's start to make our way home.

We have come full circle, or have we? In the last nine chapters, we charted new territory as we traversed through time. So many opportunities to see ourselves and one another. We took steps inward and outward. Heard the pulse of life. Danced to the heartbeat. Maybe we even cried. And hopefully we laughed out loud. Grueling and glorious. Caterpillar, cocoon, and butterfly—*all in one*.

Learning—as the practice of freedom—is not for the faint of heart. It demands the courage to love not just personally but also collectively. This is the antithesis to the work of so many school systems today. The physical, intellectual, and structural violence of toxic oppressive ecosystems. Nevertheless, inside these institutions, we are still responsible for the lives of our students. We are implicated in the work of society, not just victims of circumstance.

There is no education without educators. When we change, the system changes. This point cannot be understated. We've been banging on the wrong door! We need to turn in if we ever want to drastically reimagine schooling. Shapeshifting ourselves shapeshifts learning, not the other way around. We are sovereign, and we need to reclaim it!

We've struggled too many generations for liberation; teachers of abolition, unite! We are teaching not only to put ourselves back together but also to put the world back together. We recognize that there's no definitive teacher, only teachings on this long path. We are also here, with you, making new roads by walking.[7]

Human beings are magical.
Bios and Logos.
Words made flesh,
muscle and bone animated by hope and desire,
belief materialized in deeds,
deeds which crystallize our actualities
. . . And the maps of spring always have to be redrawn again,
in undared forms.
~ Sylvia Wynter ~

Here's how we can further materialize our spiritual potential through kinetic energy. For a real example, let's turn to our final parable. As you slowly read, notice that Khing, the master carver, calmed his inner thoughts into a single point of focus before setting out into the woods. His inner work prepared him for a *live encounter* with the tree that called forth the perfected bell stand.

The Woodcarver

Khing, the master carver, made a bell stand
Of precious wood. When it was finished,
All who saw it were astounded. They said it must be
The work of spirits.

The prince of Lu said to the master carver:
"What is your secret?"

Khing replied: "I am only a workman:
I have no secret. There is only this:
When I began to think about the work you commanded
I guarded my spirit, did not expend it
On trifles, that were not to the point.
I fasted in order to set my heart at rest.

After three days fasting,
I had forgotten gain or success.
After five days, I had forgotten praise or criticism.
After seven days I had forgotten my body with all its limbs.

By this time all thought of your Highness
And of the court had faded away.
All that might distract me from the work
Had vanished.
I was collected in the single thought
Of the bell stand.

Then I went to the forest
To see the trees in their own natural state.
When the right tree appeared before my eyes,
The bell stand also appeared in it, clearly, beyond doubt.

All I had to do was to put forth my hand
And begin.

If I had not met this particular tree
There would have been
No bell stand at all.

What happened?

> My own collected thought
> Encountered the hidden potential in the wood;
> From this live encounter came the work
> Which you ascribe to the spirits."
>
> ~ *Chuang Tzu* ~[8]

In *The Soul of Learning*, we're echoing Chuang Tzu and magnifying prophecies. Our own collected thought encountered the hidden potential of each other, and from this live encounter, we came to see the positive force of the collective process. We've sought to tap into the universal soul and the universe's electro-magnetic energy, eternally balanced, with no beginning and no end. Sheer abundance! Joining into this flow of higher energies elevates consciousness and connectivity. The power of love as a forcefield. A light so bright it can be felt in the next galaxy. It is the triumph of the human spirit.

Radiate. And pause.

Like the woodcarver who created a beautiful bell stand, we, too, are reminded that teaching is about first preparing our inner world. Once clear and focused, we are able to experience a live encounter, with ourselves, our students, and the classroom.

> *When God said, "My hands are yours,"*
> *I saw that I could heal any creature in this world;*
> *I saw that the divine beauty in each heart*
> *is the root of all time and space.*
> ~ Rabia ~

Being human is connected to anticolonial and decolonial struggles. Learning can liberate. In James Baldwin's final interview here shares:

> *I think at the bottom you have to be serious.*
> *No one can point it out to you; you have to see it yourself.*
> *That's the only way you can act on it.*
> *And when it arrives it's a great shock.*
> *It's a great shock to realize that you've been so divorced.*
> *So divorced from who you think you are—from who you really are.*
> ~ James Baldwin[9] ~

We are slowing down and want to thank you for persevering all the way to the end. We are sincerely grateful for you! What a blessing to have traveled and traversed these words with you.

We began this journey in Haridwar, one of the holiest cities in India. There in the foothills of the Himalayas, we arose early in the morning, before the sunrays had lit up the skies, and joined the beloved community in chanting the Gayatri Mantra. Dr. Chinmay Pandya teaches that the true meaning of the mantra is, "Oh, God, lead me on the right path." Agamvir, one of the elders who lives at the university, shared, "Oh, God, lead us to the right path." What a high calling. Our book seeks to serve as a living embodiment of both sources of wisdom. Individually, we need to align with our soul, which shares our deepest truth, and walk with measured steps. Altogether, we are traveling this sacred journey called life. Our power is not just in any particular words: it is in the faithfulness to integrate and practice them. As you walk in the wisdom of the work, please take these teachings with you. Along the way, may this book—as an offering to all types of educators, mentors, and guides—act as a shelter and shield that leads us toward the soul of learning.

OM
Bhur-Bhuvah Savah
Tat-Savitur-Varennyam,
Bargo, Devasya Dhiimahi
Dhiyo Yo Nah Prachdayat
OM
~ The Gayatri Mantra ~

Notes

1. Sri Aurobindo. (1997). *The Human Cycle: The Ideal of Human Unity War and Self-Determination*. Pondicherry: Sri Aurobindo, vol. 25, pp. 424–425.
2. E. Davy Pearmain, ed. (2007). *Doorways to the Soul: 52 Wisdom Tales from Around the World*. Eugene, OR: Resource Publications, pp. 71–72.
3. Public writing of Shri Ram Archarya, the main teacher/guru who began Shantikunj and created the vision for Dev Sanskriti University DevSanskriti.org.
4. From Serotiny: The Story of Lead to Life on Vimeo.
5. https://unitedplayaz.org.
6. www.leadtolife.org.
7. P. Freire & Horton, M. (1990). *We Make the Road Walking: Conversations on Education and Social Change*. Philadelphia, PA: Temple University Press.
8. "The Woodcarver," T. Merton, trans. (1997). *The Way of Chuang-Tzu*. New York: A New Directions Book, pp. 110–111.
9. J. Baldwin. (2014). *James Baldwin: The Last Interview and Other Conversations*. Brooklyn, NY: Melville House Publishing, p. 87.

AFTERWORD

As a history teacher, cultural activist, and professional educator of over 30 years, with experience both in and outside of schools, I recognize in this book, *The Soul of Learning*, a deep provocation to seek Peace in the world, in our interactions, and within ourselves.

It's important to acknowledge that I was Vajra's teacher. I watched her grow from a child of consciousness into a scholar. Although I met her in the schoolhouse (in the Black Studies Department at Berkeley High, to be exact), her ability to study reached far beyond the classroom. She was a young white girl trying to find her way in a racist society. As her teacher, I had a responsibility to her awakening. Our paths have been connected ever since. Now, this book that Mary and Vajra crafted provides a roadmap to liberated learning. It is personal, pedagogical, and prophetic.

I am the son, grandson, and great grandson of educators. Any place where divine instruction finds a platform is an initiation for me to celebrate life, and to reflect and embody my work. Recognizing the divine in others shines a mirror on my own divinity. In that reflection, even in the reach for Peace, I don't always like what I see.

Pieces of my ancestors are in me, and I carry their story and legacy forward through time like a baton in an omni temporal race. In so many ways, this book that was crafted by Mary and Vajra felt to me like fragments of a baton strategically reconstituted so another generation can carry the wisdom forward, holding stories that transcend the cultures and civilizations from which they come offers extraordinary lessons and teachings for any Peace seeker.

This book is both timely and timeless. It is about Peace. A book of Peace and for Peace.

Where does Peace exist today? For you, in this moment, and for the larger world?

We are the world we are creating. As I write this, Israeli forces are firing tear gas canisters and using live bullets inside the third most sacred place in all of Islam.

Palestinians are throwing rocks like some 21st century David, facing down tanks, bullets, and a military Goliath who believes occupation is the manifest destiny of the Israeli people. Yesterday this violence took the lives of 10 Palestinian children.

Like the authors share with us, it's a "meditation in mourning."

Peace is elusive, especially under settler colonial conditions. When the Navajo people are asked to consider Peace, they speak of restitution, recovery, remembering what they have lost, who they have lost, and who it was lost to. The Navajo find Peace in their homeland, in the very earth itself where their ancestors walked, danced, prayed, and raised families—the earth that used to feed them. Their Peace interrupted by incessant greed and an unquenchable desire for power. Uranium extracted from their ancestral lands was put inside of bombs and dropped over Hiroshima and Nagasaki. Their sacred land of Peace used to rain war on others and extend the reign of war on the earth.

Like the authors share with us, Peace is within reach, and according to the *The Isha Upanishad*, "The Lord is enshrined in the hearts of all."

Peace is possible when you are whole, but when you are divided into pieces, Peace is hard to find and not generative. Like Isis trying to repair the body of her beloved. We are broken. In putting our internal pieces back together, we discover we can reconstitute most of ourselves but must also fashion Peace to make a new generation possible.

Peace is not made from the fabric of captivity nor by those who maintain war. It is of the earth itself—fashioned out of what we have lost, petrified, and forgotten. Even in the deepest personal moments of sacred reflection, what we fashion is not of us; it is beyond us. Yet here we are searching for trees to sit under and meditate on future possibility, except the trees are on fire or full of police. Hard to meditate under occupation. Hard to find Peace when you can be justifiably shot in your own home.

Hard for Peace to live where Justice does not.

This is not about Israel or Palestine, nor is this about the American empire, and though I fit the description, this is not about Breonna Taylor, or Stephon Clarke, or George Floyd. This is not a hit piece or some tool to disturb Peace; this is in fact an Affirmation of Peace and a hope that everyone who has the space and time and opportunity to do so . . . breathes! This book points us toward inner and outer breathing and being. It encourages others to give people space and time to breathe, to settle the waters and find Peace within themselves. Like water, air, and sunshine—like life itself—we believe Peace should be the right for everyone on earth.

Can I pray in Peace?
Can I breathe in Peace?
Can I sleep in Peace?
Can I parent in Peace?
Can I run in Peace?
Can I be in Peace?

Unfortunately, Peace is often treated as a privilege, where sanctuary is defined as administrative leave, as occupied territory, where Peace has to be protected and served by officers. For too many, Peace is earned by compliance, submission, and subordination. Peace is seen as the right of the colonizer, the occupier, those in power, even when kneeling on someone's neck, or teaching someone misinformation, or justifying violent mobs.

Is peace the responsibility of the colonized, the occupied, those under power, even when laying prone and breathless under someone's knee? They don't have a right to Peace? They have a responsibility to be peaceful in their protest against occupation, peaceful while they suffocate under the choke hold of their protectors? Even when the bones of their grandparents are disturbed, unearthed, and scattered under housing developments. Even when the bones of their murdered children are used to teach classes about bones.

Even while in a mosque with family, during a holy month of Ramadan, teaching your child how to pray or how not to fall prey, you do not deserve Peace? You deserve tears, you deserve to choke, gasp for breath, you deserve rubber bullets shot in your eyes, you deserve blindness because the Peace you seek will never be found. On this land, on this ground, it seems to always belong to someone else, to those who can afford to wield it against others, to those who believe they deserve to be served.

Prey or Pray. Piece or Peace. What do we want? What are we teaching?

The Soul of Learning charts a different way forward. Altering our very axiology.

In many of the major religions of the world, suffering is a theme. Overcoming suffering, enduring suffering, accepting suffering—the theme varies in its application but seems to be a prerequisite of Peace. The recognition of injustice is a first step to rectifying it. Recognizing inequity is the first step to addressing it. When injustice is denied, Peace is impossible. When inequity is justified, Peace becomes even more elusive.

So as a first step and a last step in finding the Peace within yourself, find ways to be in harmony with Peace seekers who seek out injustice, identify harm, and recognize suffering. And commit to discovering the ways to end it in yourself, in others, and in the world.

Breathe this: *Injustice anywhere is a threat to justice everywhere.*
Meditate on this: *Injustice anywhere is a threat to justice everywhere.*
Chant this: *Injustice anywhere is a threat to justice everywhere.*
Walk this: *Injustice anywhere is a threat to justice everywhere.*
Be this: *Know justice, Know Peace.*

Hodari Bayano Davis, Ed.M.
Ph.D. candidate, UC Davis School of Education
Former National Program Director of Youth Speaks
Founding Partner of Edutainment for Equity

REFERENCES

AuQ1

Adams, D. W. (1995). *Education for Extinction: American Indians and the Boarding School Experience, 1875–1928*. St. Lawrence, KS: University Press of Kansas.
Amrine, M. (1946). "The Real Problem is in the Hearts of Men." *New York Times Magazine*, June 23.
Apple, M. W. (1995). *Education and Power*. London: Routledge.
Bache, C. M. (2004–2005). "High Octane Learning." *Shift: At the Frontiers of Consciousness*, 5, 35–36.
Bache, C. M. (2008). *The Living Classroom: Teaching and Collective Consciousness*. Albany, NY: SUNY Press.
Bailey, K. (2019). *Sol Affirmations: A Tool Kit for Reflection and Manifesting the Light Within*. New York: Self-Published.
Bark, C. (1995). *Rumi*. San Francisco: Harper.
Bauman, L., ed. (2004). *The Gospel of Thomas: Wisdom of the Twin*. Ashland, OR: White Cloud Press.
Bly, R., trans. (1977). *The Kabir Book: Forty-Four of the Ecstatic Poems of Kabir*. Boston: Beacon Press, A Seventies Press Book.
Boggs, G. L. (2007). *Opening Ceremony at the Allied Media Conference in Detroit Michigan*. https://amc.alliedmedia.org/.
Bourdieu, P., Passeron, J. C. & Nice, R. (1977). *Education, Society and Culture*, trans. R. Nice. London: Sage.
Bourgeault, C. (2008). *The Wisdom Jesus*. Boston, MA: Shambhala.
Bowles, S. & Gintis, H. (1976). *Schooling in Capitalist America: Educational Reform and the Contradictions of Economic Life*. New York: Basic Books.
Braden, G. (2017). *The Science of Self-Empowerment: Awakening the New Human Story*.
Browder, A. T. (1992). *Nile Valley Contributions to Civilization: Exploding the Myths* (Vol. 1). Washington, DC: Institute of Karmic Guidance.
Brown, J. & Isaasc, D. (2005). *The World Café: Shaping Our Future Through Conversations That Matter*. San Francisco: Berrett-Koehler.
Bruce Lee. https://us02web.zoom.us/j/81492065718?pwd=d3FUTUpyNVNQeERwRzBjZHBkREt0Zz09.

References

Buber, M. (1970). *I and Thou*. New York: Simon & Schuster.

Carew, J. & Lightfoot, S. (1979). *Beyond Bias: Perspectives on Classrooms*. Cambridge, MA: Harvard University Press.

Chatmon, C. & Watson, V. (2018). "Decolonizing School Systems: Racial Justice, Radical Healing, and Educational Equity inside Oakland Unified School District." *Voices in Urban Education*, 48.

Cherokee Legend. www.firstpeople.us/.

Chevalier, G., Sinatra, S. T., Oschman, J. L., Sokal, K. & Sokal, P. (2012). "Earthing: Health Implications of Reconnecting the Human Body to the Earth's Surface Electrons." *Journal of Environmental and Public Health*. https://doi.org/10.1155/2012/291541.

Christensen, L. & Watson, D., eds. (2015). *Rhythm and Resistance: Teaching Poetry for Social Justice*. Milwaukee, WI: A Rethinking Schools Publication.

Clarke, J. H. (1993). *African People in World History*. Baltimore, MD: Black Classic Press.

Coates, T. (2015). *Between the World and Me*. New York: Spiegel and Grau.

Coelho, P. (1998). *The Alchemist*. New York: HarperOne.

Dalton, J. E. (2018). "Embracing a Contemplative Life: Art and Teaching as a Journey of Transformation." In *The Teaching Self: Contemplative Practices and Pedagogy in Pre-Service Teacher Education*, eds. J. E. Dalton, K. Byrnes, & E. Dorman. Lanham, MD: Rowman & Littlefield.

Dalton, J., Hall, M. & Hoyser, C. (2019). *The Whole Person: Embodying Teaching and Learning Through Lectio and Visio Divina*. New York: Rowman & Littlefield.

Davy Pearmain, E., ed. (2007). *Doorways to the Soul: 52 Wisdom Tales from Around the World*. Eugene, OR: Resource Publications.

Diop, C. A. (1974). *The African Origin of Civilization: Myth or Reality*. Westport, CT: Lawrence Hill.

DuBois, W. E. B. (1903). "The Talented Tenth." *The Negro Problem: A Series of Articles by 46*. http://bible.oremus.org/?passage=Psalm+46.

Easwaran, E. (2007a). *The Bhagavad Gita*. Tomales, CA: Nilgiri Press.

Easwaran, E., trans. (2007b). *The Dhammapada*. Tomales, CA: Nilgiri Press.

Easwaran, E., trans. (2007c). *The Upanishads*. Tomales, CA: Nilgiri Press.

Evol, K. (2020). *A Garden of Black Joy: Global Poetry from the Edges of Liberation and Living*. Minneapolis, MN: Wise Ink Creative Publishing.

Ewing, E. (2017). *Electric Arches*. Chicago, IL: Haymarket Books.

Fables, A. (1909–14). "The Harvard Classics." *Bartleby.com*. www.bartleby.com/17/1/62.html.

Fanon, F. (1963). *The Wretched of the Earth*, trans. C. Farrington. London: Grove Press.

Forest, H. (1996). *Wisdom Tales from Around the World*. Little Rock, AR: August House Publishers.

Freire, P. (1970). *Pedagogy of the Oppressed*. New York: Continuum Publishing.

Freire, P. & Horton, M. (1990). *We Make the Road Walking: Conversations on Education and Social Change*. Philadelphia, PA: Temple University Press.

Gandhi, M. https://josephranseth.com/gandhi-didnt-say-be-the-change-you-want-to-see-in-the-world/.

Gebser, J. (1985). *The Ever-Present Origin*. Athens, OH: Ohio University Press, kindle edition.

Gibran, K. (1980). *The Prophet*. New York: Alfred A. Knopf.

Ginwright, S. (2015). *Hope and Healing in Urban Education: How Urban Activists and Teachers Are Reclaiming Matters of the Heart*. London: Routledge.

Givens, J. (2021). *Fugitive Pedagogy: Carter G. Woodson and the Art of Black Teaching*. Cambridge, MA: Harvard University Press.

Goldberg, M. (2015). *The Goddess Pose: The Audacious Life of Indra Devi, the Woman Who Helped Bring Yoga to the West.* Vintage. www.poemhunter.com/poem/rumi-s-silence/.
Grumbs, A. (2020). *Undrowned: Black Feminist Lessons from Marine Mammals.* Chico, CA: AK Press.
Gunnlaugson, O., Sarath, E., Scott, C. & Bai, H. (2014). *Contemplative Learning and Inquiry Across Disciplines.* Albany, NY: SUNY Press.
Gunnlaugson, O., Scott, C., Bai, H. & Sarath, E. (2017). *The Intersubjective Turn: Theoretical Approaches to Contemplative Learning and Inquiry Across Disciplines.* Albany, NY: SUNY Press.
Gunnlaugson, O., Scott, C., Bai, H. & Sarath, E. (2019). *Catalyzing the Field: Second-Person Approaches to Contemplative Learning and Inquiry.* Albany, NY: SUNY Press.
Hafiz. (1999). *The Gift of Hafiz: Poems by Hafiz The Great Sufi Master,* trans. Daniel Ladinsky. New York: Penguin.
Hanh, T. N. (2012). *Awakening of the Heart: Essential Buddhist Sutras and Commentaries.* Berkeley, CA: Parallax Press.
HeartMath Institute. www.HeartMath.org.
Helminski, K. (2017). *Living Presence.* York: Tarcher/Perigree.
Henry, D. (2014). "Stunning Health Effects of Magnetic Fields on Our Physiology." *Natural News,* June 29. www.naturalnews.com.
hooks, b. (1994). *Teaching to Transgress: Education as the Practice of Freedom.* New York and London: Routledge.
hooks, b. (2009). *Belonging: A Culture of Place.* New York and London: Routledge.
hooks, b. (2013). *Writing Beyond Race: Living Theory and Practice.* New York and London: Routledge.
Jackson, J. G. (1985). *Ethiopia and the Origin of Civilization.* Baltimore, MD: Black Classic Press.
James, W. (1890). *The Principles of Psychology* (Vol. 1). New York: Henry Holt and Co. https://doi.org/10.1037/10538-000
Jarrett, L. (2015). *Nourishing Destiny.* Stockbridge, MA: Spirit Path Press.
Jarrett, L. (2021). *Deepening Perspectives on Chinese Medicine.* Stockbridge, MA: Spirit Path Press.
Keator, M. (2017). "Reclaiming the Deep Reading Brain in the Digital Age." *Radical Pedagogy,* 14 (2), August.
Keator, M. (2018). *Lectio Divina as Contemplative Pedagogy: Reappropriating Monastic Practice for the Humanities.* London: Routledge.
Keator, M. (2019). "*Lectio Divina* and the Awakening of the Soul." In *The Whole Person: Embodying Teaching and Learning Through Lectio and Visio Divina.* New York: Rowman and Littlefield.
Keator, M. (2020a). "Human Prescencing in the Techne of a Contemplative Space." *Dev Sanskriti Interdisciplinary International,* 15, February.
Keator, M. (2020b). "World Café to Listening Café: Creating a Community of Listeners and Learners." *The Journal of Contemplative Inquiry,* 7 (1), December.
Keator, M., Savage, W. J., Foley, A., Hussein, H., et al. (2017). "Interfaith Dialogue: The Art of Listening." *The Journal of Contemplative Inquiry,* 4 (1).
Kelley, R. (2002). *Freedom Dreams: The Black Radical Imagination.* Boston, MA: Beacon Press.
Khan, H. I. (1921). *The Bowl of Saki.* Geneva, Switzerland: International Headquarters of the Sufi Movement.
Khemir, N., comp. (1996). *The Wisdom of Islam.* New York: Abbeville Press.
Kimmerer, R. (2013). *Braiding Sweetgrass: Indigenous Wisdom, Scientific Knowledge, and the Teachings of Plants.* Minneapolis, MN: Milkweed.

References

Kofman, F. (2006). *Conscious Business: How to Build Values Through Values*. Boulder, CO: Sounds True.
Laude, P. (2011–2012). "The Truth of Truths." *Parabola*, 35, Winter.
Leloup, J. Y., ed. (2005). *The Gospel of Thomas: The Gnostic Wisdom of Jesus*. Rochester, VT: Inner Traditions.
Levy, D. (2016). *Mindful Tech*. New Haven: Yale University Press.
Lewis, S. L. (1981, 2012). *The Bowl of Saki Commentary*. San Francisco: Sufi Ruhaniat International.
Lichtmann, M. (2005). *The Teacher's Way: Teaching and the Contemplative Life*. New York: Paulist Press.
Long, B. (1996). *Knowing Yourself: The True in the False*. Barry Long Books.
Love, B. (2019). *We Want to Do More Than Survive: Abolitionist Teaching the Pursuit of Educational Freedom*. Boston, MA: Beacon Press.
MacLeod, J. (1995). *Ain't No Makin' It: Leveled Aspirations in a Low-Income Neighborhood*. Boulder, CO: Westview Press.
Mayer, P. *Heaven Below*. www.petermayer.net/music.
Meadows, D. (2000). *What Does It Mean to Be Human?*, eds. F. Franck, J. Roze & R. Connolly. New York: St. Martin's Griffin.
Menakem, R. (2017). *My Grandmother's Hands*. Las Vegas, NV: Central Recovery Press.
Merton, T. (1968). *The Other Side of the Mountain: The Journals of Thomas Merton Volume 7: 1967–1968*. New York: Harper Collins.
Merton, T., trans. (1997). *The Way of Chuang-Tzu*. New York: A New Directions Book.
Miller, J. P. (2000). *Education and the Soul: Towards a Spiritual Curriculum*. Albany, NY: SUNY Press.
Mitchell, S., ed. (1993). *The Enlightened Heart: An Anthology of Sacred Poetry*. San Francisco: HarperPerennial.
Morrison, T. www.youtube.com/watch?v=n2txzMkT5Pc.
Morrison, T. (1998). *Paradise*. New York: Knopf.
Moses, J. (2002). *Oneness: Great Principles Shared by All Religions*. New York: Ballentine Books.
Native American Quotes. *Native American Wisdom Sayings: Pearls of Wisdom*. www.sapphyr.net.
Noguera, P. (2003). *City Schools and the American Dream*. New York and London: Teachers College Press.
Nurbakhsh, J. www.sufijournal.org/sufi-poetry/.
Oakes, J. (1985). *Keeping Track: How Schools Structure Inequality*. New Haven: Yale University Press.
Ober, C., Sinatra, S. T., Zucker, M., et al. (2010). *Earthing the Most Important Health Discovery Ever*. Laguna Beach, CA: Basic Health Publications.
Palmer, P. (1993). *To Know as We Are Known: Education as a Spiritual Journey*. New York and San Francisco: HarperOne.
Palmer, P. (1998). *A Hidden Wholeness*. San Francisco: Jossey-Bass.
Palmer, P. (2007). *The Courage to Teach*. San Francisco: Jossey-Bass.
Patel, L. (2016). *Decolonizing Educational Research: From Ownership to Answerability*. New York: Routledge.
Pavitra (P.B. Saint-Hilaire). (1961). *Education and the Aim of Human Life*. Pondicherry, India: Sri Aurobindo International Centre of Education.
Payne, C. & Strickland, C. S. (2008). *Teach Freedom: Education for Liberation in the African-American Tradition*. New York: Teachers College Press.
Perry, T. (1993). "The Truth of Chief Seattle, by Joyce E. Meredith and William C. Steele." Reprinted in *Pantheist Vision*, 14 (3).

References

Peters, S. (2018). *The Scholar as Human: Research and Teaching for Public Impact*, eds. A. S. Bartel & D. A. Castillo. Ithaca, NY: Cornell University Press.
Poor Richards Almanac. https://ourfriendben.wordpress.com/2008/05/04/to-thine-own-self-be-true/.
Pott, J. (1903). *Representative American Negroes of Today*. New York: J. Pott & Company.
Remer, M. (2019). "Prayer for Sacred Pauses." *Brigid's Grove*, June 15 (via Make Believe Boutique).
Rhys-Davids, T. W., trans. (2007). "The Mahaparinibbana Sutta." In *The Teachings of the Buddha*, ed. J. Kornfield. Boston: Shambhala.
Roberts, E. & Amidon, E. (2009). *Earth Prayers from Around the World: 365 Prayers, Poems and Invocations for Honoring the Earth*. New York: HarperCollins.
Rogers, J. A. (1972). *World's Great Men of Color*. New York: Macmillan Publishing Company.
Roy, A. (2016). *The End of Imagination*. Chicago, IL: Haymarket Books.
Roy, A. (2020). "The Pandemic Is a Portal." *Financial Times*, April 3. www.ft.com/content/10d8f5e8-74eb-11ea-95fe-fcd274e920ca.
Sertima, I. V. (1976). *They Came Before Columbus*. New York: Random House.
Sertima, I. V. (1992). *Golden Age of the Moor*. New Brunswick, NJ: Transaction Publishers.
Schultz, J. P. (1971). "Angelic Opposition to the Ascension of Moses and the Revelation of the Law." *The Jewish Quarterly Review*, 61 (4), 282–307.
Shakur, T. (1999). *The Rose That Grew from Concrete*. New York: Pocket Books.
Škof, L. & Berndtson, P., eds. (2018). *Atmospheres of Breathing*. New York: SUNY Press.
Star, J. (2008). *Rumi: In the Arms of the Beloved*. New York: Jeremy P. Tacher, Putnam.
Svoboda, R. (1997). *The Greatness of Saturn*. Hyderabad: Sadhana Press.
Tolle, E. (2003). *Stillness Speaks*. Emeryville, CA: New World Library.
Trimble, P. (1973). "Depatriarchalizing in Biblical Interpretation." *Journal of the American Academy of Religion*, 41 (1), 30–48. JSTOR 1461386.
Trimble, P. (1986). *God and the Rhetoric of Sexuality*. Minneapolis, MN: Fortress Press.
Tuck, E. & Yang, W. (2018). *Toward What Justice: Describing Diverse Dreams of Justice in Education*. New York and London: Routledge.
Watson, V. (2012). *Learning to Liberate: Community-Based Solutions to the Crisis in Urban Education*. New York: Routledge.
Watson, V. (2013). "Censoring Freedom: Community-Based Professional Development and the Politics of Profanity." *In Equity & Excellence in Education*, 46 (3), 387–410.
Watson, V. (2017). "Life as Primary Text: English Classrooms as Sites for Soulful Learning." Invited submission for *The Journal of the Assembly for Expanded Perspectives on Learning*, 22, 16, an affiliate of the National Council of Teachers of English.
Watson, V. (2018). *Transformative Schooling: Towards Racial Equity in Education*. New York: Routledge.
Watson, V. (2019a). "Embodied Justice: We are the Divine Text." In *The Whole Person: Lectio Divina as Transformative Practice in Teaching and Learning*, eds. J. Dalton & M. Hall. Lanham: Rowman & Littlefield.
Watson, V. (2019b). "Liberating Methodologies: Reclaiming Research as a Site for Radical Inquiry and Transformation." In *Community-Based Participatory Research: Testimonios from Chicana/o Studies*, ed. N. Deeb-Sossa. Tucson: The University of Arizona Press.
Wilbur, K. (2017). *The Religion of Tomorrow*. Boston: Shambhala.
Woodson, C. G. (1933, 2006). *The Mis-Education of the Negro*. Eritrea, East Africa: The Associated Publishers.
Ziporyn, B., trans. and intro. (2009). *Zhuangzi: The Essential Writings with Selections from Traditional Commentaries*. Hackett Publishing. www.lionsroar.com/what-is-zen-buddhism-and-how-do-you-practice-it/.

INDEX

Page numbers followed by "n" indicate a note on the corresponding page.

abolition 41, 110, 114, 124
abundance 126
activist 107, 114, 117n8
Adamah (living soil) 84
agency 31, 36–37, 119
Alchemist, The (Coelho) 5
ancient futures 118–127; racial justice 123; *Tree of Sorrows* 119–125
Ant in Love 56–57
Anthem (Cohen) 76
Arie, India 7
Atman (heart-essence) 94
Atmospheres of Breathing (Peters) 21
Aurobindo, Sri 119, 127n1
authenticity 37, 68, 118; in education 1; mental state 31; personal and collective 100; to thrive, power for 87
awake/awakening/awareness 7, 10, 43, 120; ancient traditions of 5; first step on journey toward 12; responsibility and 107, 128; rituals of awakening 2, 38; Seven Factors of Awakening 26; ultimate goal of 7
Awaken the Inner Teacher (Keator) 6
axis of energy 84–86

Bache, Christopher 40, 87, 103, 105n8
Bailey, Karega 96, 105n4
Baker, Ella 1
balance 42, 83, 93, 103, 107–108, 123

Baldwin, James 4, 10n2, 63, 107, 126, 127n9
banking concept 100
Barks, C. 89n2
be/being 23, 31, 39, 60, 68, 92, 94, 111; becoming into 124; energy of 87; harmonious ways of 112; higher states of being 3; inner being 5, 61, 91; sing to 77; truth as being 68; whole being 14, 50
belonging 7, 39, 79, 113, 123
beloved community 106–116; Groundation for Rastas 109; healing 109–110; Ramadan, ninth day of 108–109; *Scales of Justice* 108; teaching love 112–114; tomorrow 110–111
Berndtson, P. 21
Berry, Devin 98
Beyoncé xi
Bhagavad Gita 35, 41
Blind Men and the Elephant, The 51, 67
Boggs, Grace Lee 6, 10n5
Bourgeault, Cynthia 79, 89n7
Bowl of Saki, The (Lewis) 79
Boyle, Greg 111
Braden, G 49
Braiding Sweetgrass 3
brain 31–32; cognitive brain 31–32; hemispheres 32; hind or reptilian brain 31; neocortex 32; prefrontal lobe 32

Index

breath/breathing 20–29, 68, 130; *Breath Inside the Breath, The* (Kabir) 24; exist 22; pause 22, 24; release 22; sutra on the full awareness of 26–27; *see also* just breathe
Brown, J. 113
Buddha/Buddhism 38, 40, 55, 92–93; *see also* Zen life
Buechner, Frederick 10n4
butterfly 80–83

Catch the Wind 35
Chandogya Upanishad, The 37
Cherokee Tale 42
Christ/Christianity, Gospel 94; Christian Desert community 35; Islam and 94
Christ's Breath, The (Hafiz) 25
Christensen, Linda 98
classroom 14, 32, 38, 40; to co-create organic generative experiences 18; earth as 83; electro-magnetic fields in 87, 100–104; energy inside 87; heart as 5; nurturing collective consciousness 39
cocoon 80, 88, 106, 124
Coelho, Paulo 5
cognitive brain (emotional intelligence) 31–32
collective practices/collaborative 18–19
community 39, 106–116, 121, 123; *see also* beloved community
compassion 1, 12, 32, 39, 42, 52, 95, 108, 112, 119–121
Confucius 50, 68
conscious/consciousness 33–34, 44–45; as agency 36–37; awareness 3; brain, mind and 31, 34; breathing and 20; classrooms nurturing 39; connectivity expanded due to 6, 126; consciousness as agency 31; deep inner stillness and 12; education today about 33; ephemeral contents within 35; incessant internal chatter 31; intuitive 111; learning and 3, 23, 87; merits of 33–34; mind and 32; mindfulness and 38; in reorienting oneself 2; truth and 68; truth-consciousness-bliss 68, 94
contemplative 2, 5, 18, 30, 33, 40, 107
cooperation 119
courage 64, 69, 95, 103–104, 124
Courage to Teach, The 96
COVID-19 pandemic 107–108
create: classroom environment for brain development 32; compassionate community xv; faith in vocation 40; hospitality 14; inner boundaries to stay in silence 14; a listening café 113–114; love in 111; natural magnetic field 85; by sovereign teacher103; space 44, 60; space between words in class 14; theories to build community 123; time for reflection, introspection, and contemplation 11
Cricket Story, The 15–18

Dance of the Soul, The (Khan) 77–78
Devi, Indra 13
Dhammapada 30, 44, 48, 92
Dharmakaya Sutra 72n13
dialogue/dialogic 35, 40, 50, 57, 100–101, 114; accurate interpretations in 57; between truth seekers and sages 68; communal sharing and 114
Difference Between Heaven and Hell, The 52
discern 30, 34, 39, 62–66, 102–103
Dispute in Sign Language 55–57
Divine Text 7, 19
Do Not Open the Door 42
D'Smoke 89, 91
DuBois, W. E. B. 5, 10n3

earth 6, 43, 67, 89n14, 122; energies 83; heaven and 92; magnetic fields of 84–86; prayer 84; sky and 108; water in 21
Easwaran, E. 47nn8, 15, 92
education 5–6; *Education and the Aim of Human Life* 112; *Education and the Soul* 5, 14; higher aspects of 97; meditation on 1–10; purpose of 5, 38; Western education systems 23
ego (*ahamkara*) 33
embody/embodiment 7, 23, 39, 61, 101, 128; of energy 86; the power of silence 13
Empty Cup, The 22
energy 112; of being and becoming 87; earth's 83; electromagnetic energies 84, 126; eternal energy 5; indescribable magnetic energy 113; in torus field 85; transformed 122
Evol, Keno 4
Exodus 106
expanding perspectives 48–59; *Ant in Love* 56–57; *Dispute in Sign Language* 55–57; *A Man, His Son, and the Donkey* 53–54;

138 Index

Red and Blue Coat 54–55; *ting* (to listen) 49–50
expert 100, 114

Fanon, F. 47n11
Fasting of the Heart, The 50
Fear (Gibran) 9–10
Fire, Water, Truth, and Falsehood 63
Forest, H. 59nn3, 5, 6, 71nn3, 4
Four Establishments of Mindfulness (Budha) 26
freedom 4, 36, 46, 84, 88, 95, 108, 111; from the cocoon 80; practice of 124; reality of 41; of sovereign teacher 96
Freire, Paulo 40, 127n7
full awareness of breathing 26–27
future 35, 102, 108, 113; *see also* ancient futures

Gandhi, M. K. 38, 69
garden/gardens 4, 51, 55, 67; *Garden of Black Joy, A* 4; regenerative garden 15; of self-discovery 36
Gayatri Mantra 127
Gebser, J. 47n9
Gibran, Kahlil 10, 74, 97, 89n1, 105n5
Ginwright, Shawn 119
Gnothi seauton (know thyself) 94
Gospel of John, The 68, 72n10
Gospel of Matthew, The 62
Gospel of Thomas, The 61, 94
gratitude xiv, 28
Groundation for Rastas 109
grow: in colonial-based school systems 4; education in 112; empowerment 36; mindfulness for 38; neuroplasticity enabling 32; not-knowing in 23; nourishment for 21; pain favoring 75; in school systems 23; seeds for 110; in silence 15; wisdom 83
Grumbs, Alexis 5
Guerra, P. 89n13
Guest House, The (Rumi) 74
Gumbs, A. P. 29n2

Hafiz 25
Hanh, Thich Nhat 29n8, 36
harmony 44, 83, 112, 113, 114, 130
Hawthorn, Nathaniel 100
heal/healing 71, 77, 79, 83, 109–110, 120, 126
healing justice 119
heart of healing 73–89; anthem 76–77; axis of energy 84–86; dancing of the soul 77–78; heart breaks 74–75; language of the heart 77; magnetic pedagogy 86–87; *The Struggle of the Butterfly* 80–83; suffering 74
Helminski, K. 3, 34, 39
hidden 7, 59–60, 70, 126
hind brain (survival) 31
home 62, 63, 82, 98–99, 101, 108, 119–120, 124
hooks, bell 123
Horton, M. 127n7
human 6–7, 14–15, 23, 26, 28, 31, 37–40, 100, 111; being human 123, 126; rely on the earth's magnetic fields 85, 87; spiritual self and 79; teaching love 112; uniqueness of 119
humility xiv, 42, 78, 84
Hussle, Nipsey 87, 92

India 7, 62, 66, 68, 94, 127
In Lak'ech 109
innate violence 2
integrate/integrative 11, 101, 111
integration 7
internal witness, power of 31, 34–36
intersubjective 6, 28, 39, 46, 50
In the Depths of Solitude: Dedicated 2 Me (Shakur) 17
Isaasc, D. 113
Isha Upanishad, The 129
Islam 94, 108, 128
I-Thou relationship 50
Iyengar, B.K.S. 46
Iyotake, Tȟatȟaŋka 23

James, William 37
Japanese Bowl 75–76
Jarrett, L. 33, 34, 47nn3, 5, 49
Jesus 92
journey into truth 60–71; beingness and truth 68; Buddhist tradition 64; commit to the search 61; discern truth 62; holding fast to truth 66; subjective truth 67; truth as subject 67; truth is revolutionary 69; truth is the ultimate manifestation 68; truth resides within 62
joy 53, 83, 92, 96, 111, 113
just breathe 20–29; importance 22; stress and 20; universal breath 22; *see also* breath/breathing
justice 1, 4, 7, 12, 50, 98, 104, 107, 130; from seeking justice to living justice 107; healing justice 119; living justice 113; racial justice 123; radical 40; social

justice 111; symbol of truth and 108; truth and 64, 108

Kabir 1, 24, 37
Keator, Mary 6, 72n15, 105n7
Khan, Hazrat Inayat 30, 78, 87, 112
Khemir, N. 59n7
Kimmerer, R. 3, 10n1
kind/kindness 49, 80–82, 84
Kingdom of God, The 8
Kofman, F. 29n7

Lamar, Kendrick 98
Lamp Unto Yourself, A 67
Laude, P. 72n8
learning 3–4, 38, 49, 112; accessability 5; communal learning process 39; experiential learning 23; introspective and interactive 103; learning fields 87; listening and 50, 53; manufactured model of 40; as the practice of freedom 124; regurgitation process and 100; relational 37; roots of 6; as a sacred act 7; through silence 14; Zen form of 23
Lectio Divina 18, 72n15
Lee, Bruce 13
lesson/lessons 15, 23, 31, 35, 40–41, 50, 52, 66, 78–80, 87, 93, 98, 119
Levy, D. 29n1
Lewis, S. L. 89n6
liberation 3–4, 7, 23, 26–27, 32, 40–41, 46, 87, 124
Lichtmann, M. 5, 14
Life Through My Eyes (Shakur) 53
light: of Divine Truth xvi; inner light 7, 61, 91, 102; love as 126; a metaphor 44; teaching as 96, 98; truth as 59, 64, 68–69
Linda Mae 98–99
listening 15, 22, 38, 49–50, 52–53, 72n15, 113–114
living classroom 39, 100–104
living justice 1, 107, 113, 121, 123
Lorde, Audre 87
Lost Jewel, The 62
love 4, 56–57, 60, 66, 71, 77, 78, 79, 82, 86, 96, 110, 111, 112–113, 121

Magic School Bus, The 39
magnetic pedagogy 84, 86–88, 98, 104, 113
Maharashi, Ramana 33
Man, His Son, and the Donkey, A 53–54
Marley, Bob 30, 36, 91, 111
Meadows, D. 59n1
meditation 1–10, 38, 43, 64, 108, 129

Menakem, Resmaa 32
mental emancipation 30–46; consciousness as agency 31, 36–37; enlightenment 44; internal witness, power of 34–36; meditation 38; mind itself 31; power of internal witness 31, 34–36; self-discovery 35; training the mind 31, 37–42; *see also* mind
Merton, T. 2, 59n2, 117n8
Miller, John P. 5, 14, 43, 47n16
mind 31–34; consciousness 33–34; *Mind* (Budha) 43; mind-at-large 33–34, 39; training the mind 31, 37–42; *see also* brain
Morrison, Toni x, xvii, xviiin5, 3
Muhammad 92
My Grandmother's Hands: Racialized Trauma and the Pathway to Mending Our Hearts and Bodies 32

neocortex brain 32
neuroplasticity 32
Nourishing Destiny 49
Nurbakhsh, Javad 25

Om 127
One Breath (Nurbakhsh) 25
Oneness 92
Only Breath (Rumi) 26
On Teaching (Gibran) 96–97

pain 48, 73–74, 76, 79, 83, 88, 96, 121; benefits of 75; *Pain* (Gibran) 73–74
Palmer, Parker 6, 89n4, 96–97, 100, 103
parable 23, 27, 42, 52, 57, 124
past 1, 3, 35, 49, 51, 67, 98, 101–102, 124
Patel, Leigh 2–3
patience 37–38, 56, 81, 95
Patterson, Sunni 33
Pavitra (Saint-Hilaire) 112
peace 10, 13–14, 17–18, 42, 62, 82, 96
Pearce, J. C. 47n2
Pearmain, E. Davy 29n4, 47nn6, 13, 59n4, 105n1, 127n2
pedagogy 6, 39, 40, 84, 86–87, 88, 91, 104
Pedagogy of the Oppressed 40
personal activity 18, 28, 45, 58, 88, 104
perspective 50, 57, 68, 79, 95, 101, 119; education 5; of others 46; *see also* expanding perspectives
Peters, John 21
Peters, S. 123
Pimper's Paradise 30
poet/poem/poetry 2, 7, 10, 16, 33, 39, 69, 100, 110, 122

power 69, 102–104; of consciousness 34; of falsehood 64; inner 46, 94; of internal witness 34–36; magnetic pedagogy 86; mental 32; of perceptions 53; sacred 10, 44; to say *No* 44; of silence 11, 13; of the cocoon 80; of unconditional love 113, 126–127; of words 30
pray/prayer 110, 121; from the heart space 77; of Moses 106; peace and 129; teaching children to 130; *Ute Prayer* 84
Prayer for Sacred Pauses (Remer) 95
preconscious mind 32
prefrontal lobe 32
present 35, 37–38, 78, 101–102, 124
Principles of Psychology 37
productive silence 14
proverb 19, 59, 92, 110, 118
Psalms of David 77
Public Enemy 34, 41
purpose 2–7, 11–14, 36–38, 40, 87, 92, 104; of breaking open of the heart 75; divine 61; education 38; learning 3, 87; in life 36; in pains of exile and torture 92; of people 2; Unity of self with 44

Question, The 93–94

Rabbi Zusya 93
Rabia 126
racism 32, 110
radical 1, 4, 6, 50, 77, 122; justice 40; vulnerability 50, 77
Ramadan, ninth day of 108–109
read/reading 1, 7, 14–15, 24, 28, 38–39, 53, 71, 82, 108, 124
Red and Blue Coat 54–55
Remer, M. 105n3
reptilian brain (survival) 31
resistance 4, 87, 98, 112
revolution 6, 9, 69–70, 96, 111, 121
Rhys-Davids, T. W 72n7
Rhythm and Resistance: Teaching Poetry for Social Justice 98
right-relationship 12, 31
ritual 3, 19, 23, 30, 71, 121
rituals of awakening 2, 30, 38
Rose That Grew from Concrete, The (Shakur) 21–24
Roy, Arundhati 1, 113
Rumi 16, 19, 20, 26, 60, 69, 74, 76, 103
Rumi's Silence (Shepherd) 16

Sacramento Area Youth Speaks (SAYS) 39
sacred 40, 44, 120; ceremony 121; education as 6–7, 10; land of Peace 129; learning as 23, 112; lessons 78; psalm 92; into schooling 4, 84; silence as 12; timelessness 11
Sanatana Dharma of India 94
sat-chitananda (truth-consciousness-bliss) 94
Scales of Justice 108
Scarlet Letter, The 100–101
Scholar as Human, The 123
school 4–6, 14, 23, 37–40, 65, 82, 84, 87, 100–102, 124
Science of Self-Empowerment: Awakening the new human story, The 49
Seattle, Chief 22
seek/seeking 3, 11, 33, 35, 57, 60–62, 65–67, 94, 107; justice 107; life 10; real 61; right answer 57; sovereignty 105; truth-seeking 62, 67, 70
Seek That (Rumi) 2
Self 6, 11, 13, 20, 33, 35, 49, 69, 79, 91–105; knowing, and becoming a sovereign teacher 96–97; sovereignty and 93–95
self-discovery 7, 35, 36, 37, 41, 61, 87, 98
Seven Factors of Awakening 26
Shakur, Assata 110
Shakur, Tupac Amaru 17–18, 21, 53, 56
Shepherd, Michael 17–18
silence 11–19, 24, 53; collective practices 18–19; essential lessons to consider 18; as language of the soul 11; moments of 11–13, 18; personal activity 18; productive silence 14; as a sacred doorway 12; *In Silence* (Rumi) 17; stillness and 12–13; as a tool of perception 13; as an unknown abyss 144
simple 1, 32, 64, 98, 100
Sitting Bull *see* Iyotake, Tȟatȟaŋka
slow/slowly 13–15, 20, 36, 40, 49, 88, 95
solution/solutionary xvii; found within 80; being 123
song/sing 18, 46, 67, 70, 77, 87, 91, 111, 122
soul 1, 96; at the center of pedagogy and community 6; dancing of the 78; education and 38; illuminated 44; importance 6; intimate relationship with 5; of learning 91, 103, 127; metaphor for 81; poetry as the language of 100; silence and 11; soul-work 95; of transformative learning 87; truth and 67; voice of 103; work of 3

Soul of Learning, The 1, 4, 6, 106, 118, 126, 130
sovereignty 44, 61, 65, 68, 87, 91–105, 98–100; *see also* teaching toward sovereignty
space 18, 20, 24, 30, 38, 41, 80, 84, 97, 103
spiritual/spirituality 1, 41, 42, 46, 65, 70, 79, 80
story 26, 35, 48–49, 56, 67, 93; *Ancient Myth, An* 66; *Blind Men and the Elephant, The* 51, 67; *Cherokee Story* 44; *Cricket Story* 15–18; *Difference Between Heaven and Hell, The* 52; *Question, The* 93; *Zen Story* 22
stress and breathing 20
subconscious mind 32
subjective truth 67
Sufi/Sufism 2, 26, 44, 78
Summer Day, The (Oliver) 8
supraconscious mind 32
Svoboda, R. 72n6

teacher 4, 124; awakening 7; of the breath 24; guiding humanity 5; of sovereignty 65, 92–93, 96–100, 103; in student outcomes 100; in training mind 37–39; training programs 40; transference between the teacher and student 78, 87
teaching toward sovereignty 91–105; knowing Self, and becoming a sovereign teacher 96–97; living classroom 100–104; sovereign teacher support the sovereignty of each student 98–100; to be sovereign is to know the Self 93–95
Temple of Delphi 94
Tesla, Nikola 84
think/thought 17, 20, 30, 43, 59, 64, 74, 125, 126; about the rhythms 11; crisis of 49; critical thinking 32, 37; in pedagogy 41
time 2, 8–10; conditioning of 37; fasting time 108; *Kairos* time 38; and space 33, 98; traverse through 124
ting (to listen) 49–50
Tolle, Eckhart 12, 123
training the mind 31, 37–42
transformation 1, 23, 95, 111, 123; inner 46; sacred 6; of Siddhartha into Buddha 92; through education 38
transformative 2–4, 105n9, 120; learning 87; teaching 113

treasure 2, 7, 28, 62, 67
Trimble, P. 89n11
True Work (Rumi) 7
truth 7, 59; in abolishing false ideas 123; inner 94; pain and 75; painful 49; quest for 113; silence as 13; suffering and 74; symbol of 108; truth-tellers 103; *see also* journey into truth
Tuck, E. 4
Tutu, Desmond 112
Two Wolves, The 42

Udàna 51
unconscious mind 32
United Playaz (UP) 121
unity: in diversity 119; Divine Unity xvi, 109; inner unity and fasting 50; pure love and 104; sacred oneness and 68; of self 44
universal breath 22
Upanishads, The 68, 94

Vedas (the True Self) 94
Veritas 63

Watching Thought (Miller) 43
water/watering 63–64; energy fields and 95; internal waters 13; as life 21; mind 46; overall health and wellness 85; peace and 129; thoughts as 36
Watson, Farid 87
Watson, Vajra M. 41, 98
What a Time to Be Alive (Healey) 8–9
Wilber, K. 59n8, 72n11
wisdom 3, 57; of bell hooks 123; education and 38; knowledge and 83; silence and 12; teacher conducting 87; in training mind 44
Wise Master, The 65
Woodcarver, The (Tzu) 125–126
World Café, The 113
worldview 37, 48–49, 53, 109, 112
wound 76
Wynter, Sylvia 124

Yang, W. 4
Yen Hui 50

X, Malcolm xvii

Zen life 22–23; breath in 24; as an experience 23; as a learning form 23
Zhuangzi 13

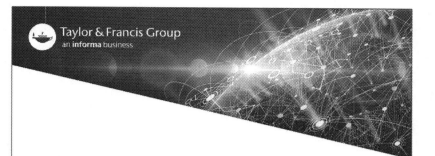

Printed in the United States
by Baker & Taylor Publisher Services